AQA

Biology

Student Workbook

Model Answers: 2010

This model answer book is a companion publication to provide answers for the exercises in the **AQA A2 Biology Student Workbook** 2010 edition. These answers have been produced as a separate publication to keep the cost of the workbook itself to a minimum, as well as to prevent easy access to the answers by students. In most cases, simply the answer is given with no working or calculations described. A few, however, have been provided with more detail because of their difficult nature.

www.biozone.co.uk

ISBN 978-1-877462-41-2

Published by BIOZONE International Ltd

BIOZONE

Additional copies of this Model Answers book may be purchased directly from the publisher

UK & EUROPE:
BIOZONE Learning Media (UK) Ltd.
Bretby Business Park, Ashby Road, Bretby,
Burton upon Trent, DE15 0YZ, **UK**
Telephone: 01283-553-257
Fax: 01283-553-258
Email: sales@biozone.co.uk

AUSTRALIA:
BIOZONE Learning Media Australia
P.O. Box 2841, Burleigh BC,
QLD 4220, **Australia**
Telephone: +61 7-5535-4896
Fax: +61 7-5508-2432
Email: sales@biozone.com.au

REST OF WORLD:
BIOZONE International Ltd.
P.O. Box 13-034,
Hamilton 3251, **New Zealand**
Telephone: +64 7-856-8104
Fax: +64 7-856-9243
Email: sales@biozone.co.nz

Contents

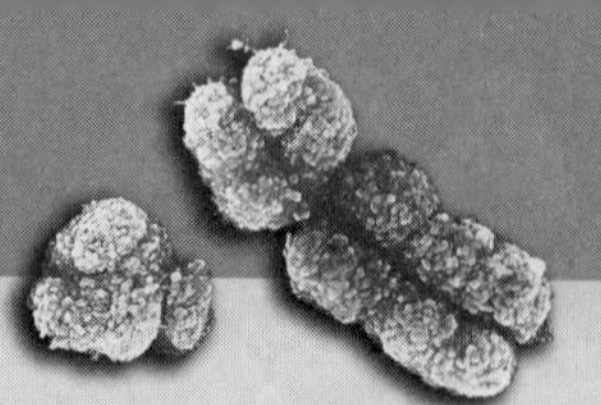

Unit 4: Populations and Environment

Investigating Populations

The Dynamics of Populations

Photosynthesis and Cellular Respiration

Energy in Ecosystems

Nutrient Cycles

Succession in Ecosystems

The Genetics of Populations

Contents

Contents

Components of an Ecosystem (page 14)

1. A **community** is a naturally occurring group of organisms living together as an ecological entity. The community is the biological part of the ecosystem. The **ecosystem** includes all of the organisms (the community) and their physical environment.

2. The biotic factors are the influences that are the result of the activities of living organisms in the community whereas the abiotic (physical) factors are the influences of the non-living part of the community, e.g. climate.

3. (a) Population (c) Community
   (b) Ecosystem (d) Physical factor

Habitat (page 15)

1. An organism will occupy habitat according to its range of tolerance for a particular suite of conditions (temperature, vegetation and cover, pH, conductivity). Organisms will tend to occupy those regions where all or most of their requirements are met and will avoid those regions where they are not. Sometimes, a single factor, e.g. pH for an aquatic organisms, will limit occupation of an otherwise suitable habitat.

2. (a) Most of a species population is found in the optimum range because this is the zone where conditions for that species are best; most of the population will select that zone.
   (b) The greatest constraint on an organism's growth within its optimum range would be intraspecific competition (or competition with different species with similar niche requirements).

3. In a marginal niche, any of the following might apply:
   - Physicochemical conditions (e.g. temperature, current speed, pH, conductivity) might be sub-optimal and create stress (therefore greater vulnerability to disease).
   - Food might be more scarce or of lower quality.
   - Mates might be harder to find.
   - The area might be more exposed to predators.
   - Resting, sleeping, or nesting places might be harder to find and/or less suitable in terms of shelter or safety.
   - Competition from other better-adapted species might be more intense.

Ecological Niche (page 16)

1. (a) The realised niche constitutes only a small proportion of the niche range which an organism can occupy. It is mainly determined by interspecific competition, so can expand or contract depending upon the level of competition at any one time.
   (b) Competition with other species may prevent the organism from exploiting all resources it is adapted to use. Competition forces species to occupy a **realised niche** that is narrower than their fundamental niche.

2. An organism will occupy habitat according to its range. Intraspecific competition tends to broaden niches as scramble competition forces individuals to move outside their optimum resource range. Interspecific competition tends to make niches narrower because it encourages niche differentiation and resource specialisation (compartmentation of the available resources) to minimise scramble competition.

Adaptations to Niche (page 17)

For each of the following the list is not exhaustive, but uses examples given on the diagrams. Note that most adaptations have components of structure, physiology, and behaviour (e.g. threat behaviours involve use of structural features. Thermoregulatory physiology involves some behaviour etc.). Categories may not be mutually exclusive.

1. **Common mole** adaptations:
   (a) **Structural**: Generally these are adaptations to aid efficient digging and tunnelling, assisting survival though protection and effective food gathering. Clawed hindfeet push soil out of the way when digging (improves efficiency). External ear openings are covered by fur to protect them when digging. Short, powerful limbs with efficient lever arrangement of muscles and joints aids rotation-thrust movement in digging. Forefeet powerfully clawed as digging tools. Velvety fur reduces friction when moving through the soil. Fur can lie in either direction so backward movement in tunnel is not hampered. Tubular body shape aids movement underground. Heavily buttressed head and neck makes tunnelling easier and more energy efficient.
   (b) **Physiological**: Well developed chemical sense aids location of food. Good sense of hearing.
   (c) **Behavioural**: Solitary and territorial behaviour (except when breeding) helps to maintain a viable food supply and reduce aggressive encounters. Sleep and feed underground offering effective protection from predators.

2. **Snow bunting** adaptations:
   (a) **Structural**: Large amount of white plumage reduces heat loss, white feathers are hollow and air filled (acting as good insulators).
   (b) **Physiological**: Lay one or two more eggs than (ecologically) equivalent species further south producing larger broods (improving breeding success), rapid moult to winter plumage is suited to the rapid seasonal changes of the Arctic.
   (c) **Behavioural**: Feeding activity continues almost uninterrupted during prolonged daylight hours (allowing large broods to be raised and improving survival and breeding success), migration to overwintering regions during Arctic winter (escapes harsh Arctic winter), will burrow into snow drifts for shelter (withstand short periods of very bad weather), males assist in brood rearing (improved breeding success).

3. (a)-(f), any six of:
   S Long, mobile ears provide acute detection of sounds from many angles (for predator detection).
   S Long, strong hind legs are adapted for rapid running (for escape from predators).
   S Cryptic/camouflage colouring of fur assists in avoiding being detected by predators.
   S Limb structure facilitates burrowing behaviour.
   P High metabolic rate and activity allows rapid response to dangers.
   P Keen sense of smell enables detection of potential threats from predators and from rabbits from other warrens (they are highly territorial).
   P Digestive system suited for coping with microbial

digestion of cellulose in the hindgut.

B European rabbit is active during any time of the day or night, but modifies its behaviour around humans to be active around dusk and dawn (crepuscular).

B Lives in groups of highly organised social structure (cooperative defence) and reduced competition between rabbits of the same warren.

B Burrows into ground to provide nesting sites, and shelter from physical conditions and predators.

B Thumps the ground with hind legs to warn others in the warren of impending danger.

4. Extra detail is (italics) provided as explanation:
   (a) Structural (*larger, stouter body conserves heat*).
   (b) Physiological (*concentrated urine conserves water*).
   (c) Behavioural (*move to favourable sites*).
   (d) Physiological (*higher photosynthetic rates and water conservation*).
   (e) Structural (*reduction in water loss*).
   (f) Behavioural and physiological (*hibernation involves both a reduction in metabolic rate and the behaviour necessary to acquire more food before hibernation and to seek out an appropriate site*).
   (g) Behavioural (*increase in body temperature*).

Sampling Populations (page 20)

1. We **sample** populations in order to gain information about their abundance and composition. Sampling is necessary because, in most cases, populations are too large to examine in total.

2. (a) Plant percentage cover: Random or systematic quadrat sampling.
   (b) Plankton density/age structure: Random or systematic point sampling (using a net or trap).
   (c) Altitudinal change in community composition: If time for sampling and analysis is constrained, a line transect with point sampling from low to high altitude. If time for sampling and analysis is less constrained, a belt transect using quadrats at regular intervals provides the most information.

3. Information about the physical environment helps to explain species distributions. Certain species are usually associated with a particular suite of physical factors (e.g. preferred exposure, temperature, humidity etc) and if these are measured and known, more information on community patterns can be gathered.

4. As the vertical distance up the trunk increases, light intensity and temperature increase and humidity declines. With these changes in physical conditions there is consequent change in the vegetation from a diverse community of shade and moisture adapted moss species, to a community comprising just one species of (hardier) tree moss and various species of lichens, i.e. species more tolerant of the microclimate of lower humidity and higher light and temperature.

Quadrat Sampling (page 21)

1. Mean number of centipedes captured per quadrat:
   Total number centipedes ÷ total number quadrats
   30 individuals ÷ 37 quadrats
   = 0.811 centipedes per quadrat

2. Number per quadrat ÷ area of each quadrat
   0.811 ÷ 0.08 = 10.1 centipedes per m^2

3. Clumped or random distribution.

4. Presence of suitable microhabitats for cover (e.g. logs, stones, leaf litter) may be scattered.

Quadrat-Based Estimates (page 22)

1. Species abundance in plant communities can be determined by using quadrats and transects, and abundance scales are often appropriate. Methods for sampling animal communities are more diverse, and density is a more common measure of abundance.

2. **Size**: Quadrat must be large enough to be representative and small enough to minimize sampling effort.

3. **Habitat heterogeneity**: Diverse habitats require more samples to be representative because they are not homogeneous.

4. (a) and (b) any two of:
   – The values assigned to species on the abundance scale are subjective and may not be consistent between users.
   – An abundance scale may miss rarer species and overestimate conspicuous ones.
   – The scale may be inappropriate for use in some habitats.
   – The semi-quantitative values assigned to the abundance categories cover a range so results will lack precision.

Sampling a Leaf Litter Population (page 23)

It must be emphasised that the actual results for this practical are not particularly important. What is of value, is learning the value and limitations of this method, preferably **before** students are asked to carry it out in a field situation. The actual results will vary, depending upon the group's agreed upon criteria for inclusion of organisms in a given quadrat (i.e. when and how an organism is counted when it is partly inside a quadrat).
Note: Some leaves are almost completely obscured by invertebrates or have other leaves on top of them.

6. Typical results for samples used are:

	Direct count	A	B	C	D
Woodlice:	89	9.5	5	13	14.5
Centipedes:	3	0	0	1	1
Springtails:	6	0	3	0	0
False scorpions:	3	1	0	1	0
Leaves:	168	29	20.5	24.5	26.5

Class results will vary depending on counting criteria.

7. Typical results for calculated density are:

	Direct count	A	B	C	D
Woodlice:	2747	1759	926	2407	2685
Centipedes:	93	0	0	185	185
Springtails:	185	0	556	0	0
False scorpions:	93	185	0	185	0
Leaves:	5185	5370	3796	4537	4907

Note: Area of 6 quadrats = (0.03 x 0.03) x 6 = 0.0054 m^2
Area of total sample area = 0.18 x 0.18 = 0.0324 m^2

8. (a) **Problems** with sampling moving organisms: Once the quadrats have been laid, the animals moving from one quadrat to another risk being counted

twice. **Solutions**: Physical barriers could be placed between each quadrat (what about the invertebrates directly underneath?). The entire area could be photographed for later analysis.

(b) Data given above. Students should be made aware of the significance of extrapolating data from a small sample. The inclusion or exclusion of single individuals may have a large effect on the density figure, particularly where the species occur in low densities. Groups could combine data to see if they get a more representative sample.

Transect Sampling (page 25)

1. (a) With belt transects of any length (10 m or more), sampling (and sample analysis) using this method is very time consuming and labour intensive.
   (b) Line transects, although quicker than belt transects, may not be representative of the community. There may be many species which are present but which do not touch the line and are not recorded.
   (c) Belt transects use a wider strip along the study area and there is much less chance that a species will not be recorded.
   (d) It is not appropriate to use transects in situations involving highly mobile organisms.
2. To test whether or not the transect sampling interval was sufficient to accurately sample the community, the sampling interval could be decreased (e.g. from a sampling interval of every 1.5 m to an interval of every 0.25 m). If no more species are detected and the trends along the transect remain the same, then the sampling interval was adequate.
3. See kite graph of the "Distribution of *Littorina*" below.

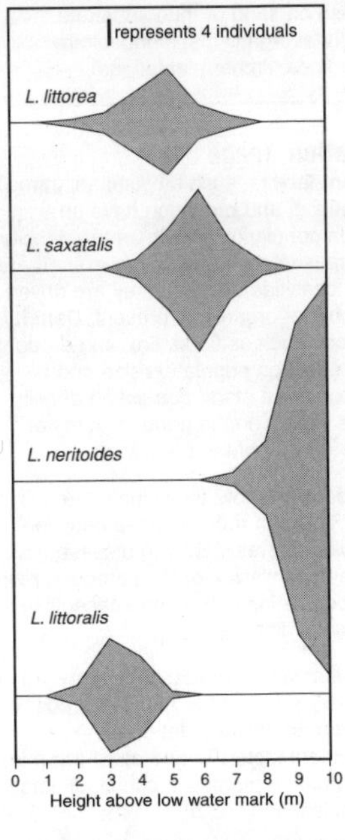

Mark and Recapture Sampling (page 27)

1. Results will vary from group to group for this practical. The actual results are not important, but it should serve as a useful vehicle for discussion of such things as sample size, variation in results between groups, and whether the method is a reliable way to estimate the size of a larger unknown group. Discussion could centre around what factors could be altered to make it a more reliable method (e.g. larger sample size, degree of mixing, increasing number of samples taken).
2. **Trout in Norwegian lake**:

Size of 1st sample:	109
Size of 2nd sample:	177
No. marked in 2nd sample:	57
Estimated total population:	109 x 177 ÷ 57 = 338.5

3. (a) Some marked animals may die.
   (b) Not enough time for thorough mixing of marked and unmarked animals.
4. (a) and (b) in any order (any two of):
   - Marking does not affect their survival.
   - Marked & unmarked animals are captured randomly.
   - Marks are not lost.
   - The animals are not territorial (must mix back into the population after release).
5. (a) Any animal that cannot move or is highly territorial (e.g. barnacle, tube worm, many mammals).
   (b) Unable to mix with unmarked portion of the population. Recapture at the same location would simply sample the same animals again.
6. (a)-(c) in any order:
   - Banding: leg bands of different color on birds.
   - Tags: crayfish shell, fish skin, mammal ears.
   - Paint/dye used to paint markings in shell/fur.
7. The scientists obtain information on fish growth to establish the relationship between age and growth. This will help manage the population to prevent overfishing. Tracking also helps to map breeding grounds and migrations so that fish can be protected at critical times in their life histories. In addition to these data, researchers will find out more about the general biology of the cod (e.g. data on feeding), which will help in the long term management and recovery of the fish stock.

Designing Your Field Study (page 29)

1. Recognising assumptions is critical to asking the appropriate questions in a study. For even the simplest of studies, some background information is important. Making some intelligent assumptions based on present knowledge allows you to focus on the questions that you really want to answer. At the same time, identifying the assumptions you have made allows you to recognise possible reasons if your results in an experiment do not support your predictions.
2. To test quadrat size it would be necessary to sample using a series of quadrats of increasing size. The cumulative number of species recorded after each successive increase in quadrat size could be plotted on a simple graph (i.e. number of species vs quadrat size). The optimum quadrat size occurs when the number of species recorded stops increasing. (<u>Note</u>: a smaller size may be accepted if you are prepared to only record dominant species. However, this always carries a risk

that trends between different areas may be missed).

3. Litter was weighed in order to quantify the weight of litter per quadrat. It is possible that the same sized quadrat contained different amounts of litter at different sites. By weighing, this is accounted for (numbers can be expressed per unit weight of litter).

4. It is possible that the presence or absence of other invertebrates may be useful in later explaining the trends observed in the millipede abundance at different sites (e.g. millipede numbers could be low where the numbers of predatory centipedes are high).

Checklist to be completed by the student.

Features of Populations (page 32)

1. (a) One of the following:
Population growth rate: If this increases (or decreases) from one time interval to the next, it indicates that the population is probably also increasing (or decreasing). **Note**: The **intrinsic** rate of population increase (r_{max}) should be distinguished from population growth rates that account for the increasing number of individuals in the population (rN). The intrinsic population growth rate is a characteristic value for each species but rN can increase rapidly as more and more individuals add to the population increase.
Total abundance: If this increases (or decreases) from one time interval to the next, it indicates that the population is also increasing (or decreasing).
Mortality: If this is increasing from one time interval to the next, it indicates that the population may be decreasing (you must also account for other sources of population change).
Birth rate & population fertility: If these increase from one time interval to the next, they indicate that the population may be increasing (you must also account for other sources of population change).
Age structure: A population dominated by young individuals is usually increasing. A population dominated by old (especially post-reproductive) individuals is usually decreasing.
(b) One of the following:
Distribution: A very clumped distribution may indicate that only some parts of the environment are suitable for supporting individuals.
Population growth and birth rates: If these are low or declining it may indicate an inability of the environment to support the population density.
Mortality: If this are very high or increasing it *may* indicate an inability of the environment to support the present population density.

2. (a) **Measurable attributes**: Density, distribution, total abundance, sex ratios, migration (sometimes difficult). In some cases, depending on the organism, also age structure and population fertility.
(b) **Calculated attributes**: Population growth rate, birth rate (natality) and death rate (mortality).

3. (a) Population sampling of an endangered species allows us to determine (any of): If population is growing and how fast; the population's age and sex structure (i.e. is it dominated by young or old, non-reproductive, individuals); population abundance, density, and distribution in different areas (habitat preference and suitability); sources of mortality (predation, disease, starvation etc.); population fertility. This information allows informed decisions to be made about the population's management.
(b) Population sampling of a managed fish species allows us to determine the population growth rate. This is critical to establishing the level of fishing that can be supported by the population (the sustainable harvest) without irreversible population decline. The growth rate is calculated taking into account population abundance, and birth and death rates. Sustainable harvest can be built into the equation as one of the (controllable) sources of mortality.

Density and Distribution (page 33)

1. (a) Resources such as food and shelter are not usually spread through the environment in an even manner. Organisms will clump around these resources.
(b) Some organisms group together for protection from the physical environment or from predators, or for the purposes of reproduction. Clumped distribution may also result from the dispersal method, especially in plants where reproduction may occur by seeds (widely dispersed) or vegetative methods.

2. Territorial behaviour whereby the establishment and demarcation of an area distributes individuals uniformly.

3. Resources are limited but distributed uniformly.

4. (a) **Clumped**: Many marine gastropods, colonial birds (seasonally), many mammals that exhibit grouping/ herd behaviour, schooling fish, colonial insects, many other invertebrates such as coral, some plants with limited dispersal.
(b) **Random**: Weed plants with effective dispersal method, shellfish on sand or mud substrate.
(c) **Uniform**: Territorial organisms, monoculture plantings (e.g. crops, timber plantations).

Population Regulation (page 34)

1. **Density dependent** factors, such as disease, parasitic infestation, competition, and predation have an increasing effect on population growth as the density of the population increases; their effects are exacerbated at high population densities because they are driven in part by the number of organisms present. **Density independent** factors, such as flood, fire, and drought have a controlling effect on population size and growth that is independent of the population density. The severity of the impact on the population is not correlated with the density of the population.

2. When population density is low, individuals are well spaced apart. This can reduce stress between individuals (improving the resistance to diseases) as well as making the transmission of the pathogen more difficult. Crowded populations are more susceptible to epidemics of infectious disease.

3. (a) Density dependent factor: Predation (e.g. by ladybird beetles), competition with other aphids for position on the best part of the plant to feed.
(b) Density independent factor: Temperature (drop in temperature in autumn months in cooler climates causes the population to crash).

Population Growth (page 35)

1. (a) Mortality: Number of individuals dying per unit time (death rate).
   (b) Natality: Number of individuals born per unit time (birth rate).
   (c) Immigration: Individuals moving into the population.
   (d) Emigration: Individuals moving out of the population.
   (e) Net migration rate: Net change in population size per unit time due to immigration and emigration.

2. (b) A declining population: B + I < D + E
   (c) An increasing population: B + I > D + E

3. USA: + 1.0 Mexico: + 3.3

4. (a) Birth rate = 14 births ÷ 100 total number of individuals x 100 % = 14% per year
   (b) Net migration rate = 2% per year
   (c) Death rate = 20% per year
   (d) Rate of population change: birth rate – death rate + net migration rate = 14 – 20 + 2 = –4% per year
   (e) The population is **declining**.

5. Limiting factors to human population growth: availability of food or land (to live or grow food), prevalence of disease and ability of public health system to prevent and treat it.

Population Growth Curves (page 36)

1. As population numbers increase, the resistance of the environment (to further population increase) increases. This constrains the population to keep to a size that the environment can support at any one time.

2. Environmental resistance refers to all the limiting factors that together act to prevent further population increase (achievement of intrinsic rate of population increase, r_{max}).

3. (a) The maximum population size (of a species) that can be supported by the environment.
   (b) The carrying capacity of an environment is determined by the availability of resources. Those that are limiting will determine the carrying capacity regardless of there being plentiful resources of other types. For example, a land area might contain enough suitable habitat to accommodate 10 breeding pairs of seed eating birds, but if nitrogen availability limits primary productivity to a level that provides enough food for only 5 breeding pairs, then nitrogen is the limiting factor determining the carrying capacity in that instance.

4. (a) A new introduction increases exponentially (or nearly so) in a new area because its niche in that environment is unexploited up to that point. Resources (food, space, shelter etc.) are plentiful and readily available. The population rapidly increases, then slows as the population encounters environmental resistance.
   (b) Population numbers would fluctuate around some relatively stable population size that equates to what the environment can support (the carrying capacity).

5. High rabbit densities can lower the carrying capacity of environments by reducing the ability of the environment to recover from the impacts of extra grazing pressure. In Britain, the grasslands have had a long history of exposure to rabbits, whose grazing pressure helped to maintain grasslands and prevent the invasion of shrubs.

Note: Low rabbit densities (as opposed to total absence) are now seen as desirable in that they maintain some grasslands (e.g. chalk grasslands) and allow many invertebrate species (dependent on grassland herbs) to survive.

Species Interactions (page 37)

1. (a) **Mutualism** between a ruminant and its gut microflora: In this relationship, both parties benefit (in this case, more than two species are involved, as several microbial species are mutualistic with the ruminant). Volatile fatty acids, released as a result of microbial digestion of cellulose, provide a source of energy for the ruminant (e.g. cow, goat, sheep, deer). The microbes themselves are also digested and this provides protein. The microbes (usually a species specific combination of bacteria and ciliates) gain an oxygen free, nutrient rich environment at the optimum growing temperature.
   (b) **Commensalism** between shark and remora: In this relationship, the commensal (the remora) benefits by being transported in relative safety with very little energy cost to itself. The shark (various species have commensal remoras) is neither benefitted nor disadvantaged by the remora's presence.
   (c) **Parasitism** between tapeworm and humans: In this relationship, the tapeworm parasite (*Taenia solium*) gains by having a safe, equable environment in which to live and produce proglottids (reproductive segments), and by having a readily available supply of nutrients from the digested slurry in the host's gut. Even the proglottids are specialised for the selective absorption of digested food. The human host is harmed by the loss of nutrients to the parasite, and by gut irritation and potential infection.
   (d) **Parasitism** between a cat flea and its host: In this relationship, the flea (*Ctenocephalides* spp.) is the parasite and gains by having a relatively safe environment at the right temperature in which to live and produce eggs, and by having a readily available supply of nutrients in the form of the cat's blood. The cat host (*Felis domestica*) is harmed to an extent by blood loss, but more by skin irritation and infection (including flea allergy dermatitis), and by the transmission of other parasites, such as tapeworms, which are transmitted by the flea.

2. Interactions:

	B	**Description**
(a)	+	Both species benefit.
(b)	0	Species A benefits, no effect on species B.
(c)	+	Species A (the host) is harmed, species B (the parasite) benefits.
(d)	–	No effect on species A, species B is harmed.
(e)	+	Species A (prey) is harmed, species B (the predator) benefits.
(f)	–	Both species (competitors) are harmed.
(g)	–	Species A (herbivore) benefits, species B (plant) is harmed.
(h)	–	Species A benefits, species B is harmed. Species A is unaffected, species B is harmed.

3. Identifying examples of species interactions:

Term	A	B
(b) Exploitation	+	–
(c) Antibiosis (or amensalism)	0	–
(d) Competition	–	–
(e) Commensalism	+	0
(f) Mutualism	+	+

Intraspecific Competition (page 39)

1. (a) **Individual growth rate**: Intraspecific competition may reduce individual growth rate when there are insufficient resources for all individuals (Examples: tadpoles, *Daphnia*, many mammals with large litters). **Note**: Individuals compete for limited resources and growth is limited in those individuals that do not get access to sufficient food.
   (b) **Population growth rate**: Intraspecific competition reduces population growth rate. Examples as above. **Note**: Competition intensifies with increasing population size and, at carrying capacity, the rate of population increase slows to zero.
   (c) **Final population size**: Intraspecific competition will limit population size to a level that can be supported by the carrying capacity of the environment. **Note**: In territorial species, this will be determined by the number of suitable territories that can be supported.
2. (a) They reduce their individual growth rate and take longer to reach the size for metamorphosis.
   (b) Density dependent.
   (c) The results of this tank experiment are unlikely to represent a real situation in that the tank tadpoles are not subject to normal sources of mortality and there is no indication of long term survivability (of the growth retarded tadpoles). **Note**: At high densities, many tadpoles would fail to reproduce and this would naturally limit population growth (and size) in the longer term.
3. Reduce intensity of intraspecific competition by:
   (a) Establishing hierarchies within a social group to give orderly access to resources.
   (b) Establishing territories to defend the resource within a specified area.
4. (a) Carrying capacity might decline as a result of unfavourable climatic events (drought, flood etc.) or loss of a major primary producer (plant species).
   (b) Final population size would be smaller (relative to what it was when carrying capacity was higher).
5. **Territoriality** is a common consequence of intraspecific competition in mammals and birds. In any habitat, resources are limited and only those with sufficient resources will be able to breed. This is especially the case with mammals and birds, where the costs of reproduction to the individual are high relative to some other taxa. Even though energy must be used in establishing and maintaining a territory, territoriality is energy efficient in the longer term because it gives the breeding pair relatively unchallenged access to resources. As is shown in the territory maps of golden eagles and great tits, territories space individuals apart and reduce intraspecific interactions. The size of the territory is related to the resources available within the defended area; larger territories are required when resources are poorer or widely dispersed. As is shown by the great tit example, when territory owners are removed, their areas are quickly occupied by birds previously displaced by competition.

Interspecific Competition (page 41)

1. The two species have similar niche requirements (similar habitats and foods). Red squirrels once occupied a much larger range than currently. This range has contracted steadily since the introduction of the greys. The circumstantial evidence points to the reds being displaced by the greys.
2. The greys have not completely displaced the reds. In areas of suitable coniferous habitat, the reds have maintained their numbers. In some places the two species coexist. **Note**: It has been suggested that the reds are primarily coniferous dwellers and extended their range into deciduous woodland habitat in the absence of competition.
3. Habitat management allows more effective long term population management *in-situ* (preferable because the genetic diversity of species is generally maintained better in the wild). Reds clearly can hold their own in competition with greys, provided they have sufficient resources. **Enhancing the habitat** preferred by the reds (through preservation and tree planting), assists their success as a competing species. Providing **extra suitable food plants** also enables the reds to increase their breeding success and maintain their weight through winter (thus entering the breeding season in better condition).
4. Other conservation strategies to aid red squirrel populations could include (any of): Captive breeding and release of reds into areas where they have been displaced, control/cull of grey squirrels (particularly in habitats suitable for reds), transfer of reds from regions where populations are successful to other regions of suitable habitat, supplementary feeding prior to the breeding season, public education to encourage red squirrels over greys.
5. (a) A represents the **realised niche** of *Chthamalus*.
   (b) When *Balanus* is removed from the lower shore, the range of *Chthalamus* extends into areas previously occupied by the *Balanus*; *Balanus* normally excludes *Chthamalus* from the lower shore.
6. Features will depend on the example chosen. Typical examples for two species that are proving to be invasive in many countries worldwide are described:
   (a) **Mallard duck** (*Anas platyrhynchos*):
   – Clutch size is relatively large compared with many other duck species.
   – Mallards are sexually aggressive and are capable of interbreeding with several native duck species where their ranges come to overlap (grey ducks in New Zealand, American black duck, the Florida mottled duck, and the endangered Hawaiian duck).
   – Mallards bully native duck species in competition for food and nest sites.
   – Mallards are adaptable in different environments.
   (b) **Mosquito fish** (*Gambusia affinis*):
   – Prolific breeders in many diverse environments.
   – Aggressive competitors for food.
   – Generalist feeders, and will prey on the eggs and larvae of native fish and frogs.
   – Reproductive strategies tuned to maximizing

reproductive output. Females are able to store sperm for extended periods and colonise environments without needing to meet a mate there.

Niche Differentiation (page 43)

1. (a) Different species may exploit different microhabitats within the ecosystem (e.g. tree trunks, leaf litter, lower or upper canopy).
   (b) Different species may exploit the same resources but at different times of the day or year.
2. Competition is avoided by the birds exploiting slightly different parts of the eucalypt habitat, with the birds feeding in different ways and/or on different food types.
3. Each damselfish exploits different parts of the reef crest and slopes as well as feeding on different food supplies and/or at different times of the day.

Predator-Prey Strategies (page 44)

1. Students could choose any of a number of examples, e.g. musk oxen defence of young, meerkat lookouts and group defence of territory, primate group vigilance etc. Examples should discuss both structural and behavioural adaptations, including (as appropriate), adaptations for escape, warning, and/or attack, and cooperative group behaviour in maintaining surveillance of the group, in warning, and (in some species) in actively defending the young.
2. Students could choose any of a number of examples, e.g. lions hunting and social canids (e.g. wolves) hunting. Examples should discuss structural adaptations for prey capture and emphasise (as appropriate) the importance of cooperative group behaviour in selecting, isolating, and capturing prey.
3. In advertising the fact that they are unpalatable, predators quickly learn to associate the colouration with distastefulness. When seen, poisonous species are not mistaken for palatable species and they are left alone.
4. Deceptive markings, such as fake eyes can momentarily, deceive predators into thinking that they are faced with a larger animal than is really the case. This may give time for the prey to escape or may result in the predator attacking a non-vital part of the prey.
5. The Batesian mimic benefits because predators universally avoid attacking animals with the same warning colouration, poisonous or not. Note: **Batesian mimicry** describes the situation when a harmless species mimics the colouration and behaviour of a poisonous species. Generally the poisonous species is unaffected by the mimicry, but for this strategy to be successful, mimics should not outnumber poisonous individuals.
6. Freezing i.e. lying low to the ground and remaining very still can enable a prey species to avoid detection.

Predator-Prey Interactions (page 45)

1. (a) Usually between about 3 and 7 years (especially for pronounced peaks), although sometimes as great as a full 10 year cycle. Note that the peaks often appear to be superimposed or the lynx peaks appear to be ahead of the hare peaks; the lynx are responding to the earlier peaks in hare abundance.
   (b) Lynx are top predators, with longer reproductive times and generation times than hares. When the hare populations increase there is a considerable time delay before this increase in available food is translated into higher population growth rates in lynx (birth rates must increase, usually mortality rates must also fall). Likewise, a fall in hare numbers takes some time to be registered by a decline in lynx population growth rate.
2. Hares are the principal food item for lynx in this system; there is little opportunity for prey switching (few alternative prey). The lynx cycles follow those of the hares closely with a similar periodicity.
3. (a) When the supply of palatable food declines, birth rates decline (adults are less well nourished and litters are smaller) and the mortality rate increases (more deaths due to starvation and disease as a result of malnutrition). **Note**: Population growth rates depend on both birth and death rates: ($r = b–d$). When natality declines and mortality increases, r becomes negative and the population declines.
   (b) High mortality (losses from the population) can be sustained by species such as rodents and lagomorphs as long as they can maintain their intrinsically high birth rates. Declines in palatable food adversely affects their ability to do this.

Population Age Structure (page 46)

1. (a) 3:1
   (b) Other factors besides changes in age structure can affect population growth, e.g. sex ratios, population fertility, and migration.
2. Over a short duration, the large cohort of prereproductive individuals will reach reproductive age and the population will continue to grow. Even if the rate of population growth continues to slow it will take several generations before the 'bulge' of reproductive individuals moves into the post-reproductive phase.
3. The age structure of England's population is not dominated by younger (pre-reproductive) individuals. Specifically, there are a large proportion of individuals at or near the end of their reproductive life and a relatively smaller number of younger individuals moving in to the reproductive age groups when they can contribute to population growth. This will keep the population at or near replacement level, but not expanding.

World Population Growth (page 47)

1. (a) Africa
   (b) Poor education on family planning. Entrenched cultural practices (large families are desirable).
2. The increased mechanisation of agriculture and move away from subsistence farming has reduced the need for large numbers of rural workers and encouraged the move of people to cities.

3. Urbanisation, particularly when it occurs rapidly without time for adequate planning, produces a number of problems including:
   - problems with adequate provision of food, water, sanitation, housing, jobs, and basic services (such as health care and education).
   - the rapid and unplanned growth of slum or squatter areas that develop on the fringes of cities. These areas often grow rapidly in response to immigrant influxes.
   - increased levels of pollution as a direct or indirect result of increased population pressure.
   - rapid spread of diseases through high density and/ or improperly serviced areas.
   - increased crime, particularly in high density, impoverished parts of cities.

Survivorship and Life Expectancy (page 49)

1. Life expectancy is a measure of the number of years a person is expected to live for at any give age. It is based on the probability of living to the next year of life. Different stages of life leave people more vulnerable than others, so life expectancy changes as one moves through these areas of life. A new born baby is highly vulnerable and has a lower life expectancy than a one year old. An 80 year is also vulnerable and has a low life expectancy. However a 90 year has a relatively high life expectancy as people who reach this age tend to then live a number of years longer.

2. As GDP increases so too does the life expectancy of the population. The curve levels out at a GDP of around 30,000 US dollars per capita.

3. Infant mortality rate is linked to a country's GDP because wealthy countries tend to have better medical support and public health infrastructure than poorer countries. This means that even infants with serious medical problems at birth are more likely to survive due the care they are likely to receive. Better education of parents and better infant nutrition are also factors in the survival of infants in high GDP countries.

4. Countries vary markedly in their living conditions and quality of life. These are two major factors in determining he survivorship of people. Countries where war and sanitation are problems have lower survivorship of their citizens.

5. (a) 78 (b) 70 (c) 63

Human Demographics (page 50)

1. Diagram C corresponds to stage one of the DTM. The wide base of the pyramid indicates a large number of under 15s (pre-reproductive) but the sides of the pyramid are steep and not many live to old age, so death rates are high. The combination of high birth rates (many children) and high death rates means the population numbers are largely stationary.

2. In less economically developed nations (LEDN), children are required to contribute to the household economy by helping with work and raising younger siblings. In more economically developed nations (MEDN), the household income is more likely to come from outside industry (i.e. wage and salary earning rather than farming, herding animals, or making crafts to sell for example) so extra children become a cost to the household rather than contributors in their own right. This is especially the case because the costs of child rearing (education, clothing, transport etc) are higher in MEDN.

ATP in Metabolism (page 52)

1. Respiration provides the source of ATP which is required for metabolic processes.

2. (a) Mitochondria provide the environment (membrane-bound enzymes and enzymes for the Krebs cycle) within which the oxygen-requiring reactions of cellular respiration can occur.
   (b) Compartmentalisation promotes functional efficiency because specific enzyme-controlled reactions occur only in particular regions and the required enzymes are located close together in an orderly way. Enzymes are then produced only in the regions where they are required. Compartmentalisation also facilitates close control of the enzyme reaction rate because the rate of entry and exit of substrates and end-products into and out of the cell or organelle can be more easily regulated.

3. The metabolic processes that assist in thermoregulation (muscular activity, sweating etc) are energy requiring (require ATP in order to proceed), making thermoregulation an energy-expensive process.

The Role of ATP in Cells (page 53)

1. In the presence of the enzyme ATPase, ATP is hydrolysed to produce ADP plus a free phosphate, releasing energy in the process.

2. Glucose

3. Cellular respiration; strictly oxidative phosphorylation.

4. Solar energy

5. Food (gaining nutrient from plants and other animals).

6. Like a rechargeable battery, the ADP/ATP system toggles between a high energy state and a low energy. The addition of a phosphate to ADP recharges the molecule so that it can be used for cellular work.

7. **PHOTOSYNTHESIS**
   Starting materials: carbon dioxide, water (as a source of hydrogens), in the presence of light and chlorophyll.
   Waste products: oxygen, water.
   Role of hydrogen carriers: NADP: Carries hydrogen between light dependent and light independent phases (where the hydrogen is incorporated into sugars).
   Role of ATP: Produced in the light dependent phase and used in the light independent phase to make sugars from carbon dioxide and hydrogen.
   Overall biological role: Uses light energy to fix carbon into organic molecules which become part of the energy available in food chains.

   CELLULAR RESPIRATION
   Starting materials: organic molecules (ultimately glucose), oxygen.
   Waste products: carbon dioxide, water.
   Role of hydrogen carriers: NAD: Carries hydrogens

to the electron transport system where their transfer between carriers is coupled to ATP production.
Role of ATP: A small amount of ATP is used initially to produce pyruvate from glucose. Produced in glycolysis, Krebs cycle, and the ETS.
Overall biological role: The process by which organisms break down energy rich molecules to release energy in a usable form (ATP).

Plants as Producers (page 54)

1. (a) water + carbon dioxide (in the presence of light and chlorophyll) → glucose + oxygen + water
   (b) $12H_2O + 6CO_2 \rightarrow C_6H_{12}O_6 + 6O_2 + 6H_2O$
2. Importance of photosynthesis (in any order):
   (a) Transforms light energy into chemical energy available to food chains.
   (b) Creates organic molecules used as building blocks for creating more complex molecules.
   (c) Releases free oxygen into the atmosphere; required by many other life forms.
3. Algae are producers and need to remain in the euphotic zone; the zone where there is enough light penetration for photosynthesis to occur (0-30 m).
4. • Oxygen becomes in shorter supply.
   • Carbon dioxide levels in the atmosphere build up with fewer plants around to act as carbon sinks.
   • Climate warms progressively.

Photosynthesis (page 55)

1. (a) Grana: Membranes that contain chlorophyll and are the site of the light dependent phase of photosynthesis. The biochemical process involves energy capture via photosystems I and II.
   (b) Stroma: The liquid interior of the chloroplast in which the light independent phase takes place. The biochemical process involves carbon fixation via the Calvin cycle.
2. (a) Carbon dioxide: Comes from the air (via stomata) and provides carbon and oxygen as raw materials for the production of glucose. Some oxygen molecules contribute to the production of H_2O
   (b) Oxygen: Comes from CO_2 gas (via stomata) and H_2O (via the roots and vascular system). The oxygen from the CO_2 is incorporated into glucose and H_2O. The oxygen from the water is given off as free oxygen (a waste product).
   (c) Hydrogen: Comes from water (via the roots and vascular system) obtained from the soil. This hydrogen is incorporated into glucose and H_2O.
   Note: The clarify: isotope studies show that the carbon and oxygen in the carbohydrate comes from CO_2, while the free oxygen comes from H_2O.
3. Scientists use isotopes to tag molecules taken up by plants and analyse the products produced as a result of photosynthesis. For example, the use of oxygen isotopes can identify the origin of the free oxygen released in photosynthesis:
   $CO_2 + 2H_2{}^{18}O \rightarrow [CH_2O] + {}^{18}O_2 + H_2O$
4. Glucose is used as the fuel for cellular respiration, or used to construct cellulose, starch, or disaccharide molecules (e.g. fructose). Oxygen is required for aerobic respiration and water is recycled and even reused for photosynthesis.

Pigments and Light Absorption (page 56)

1. The absorption spectrum of a pigment is that wavelength of the light spectrum absorbed by a pigment, e.g. chlorophyll absorbs red and blue light and appears green. Represented graphically, the absorption spectrum shows the relative amounts of light absorbed at different wavelengths.
2. Accessory pigments absorb light wavelengths that chlorophyll *a* cannot absorb, and they pass their energy on to chlorophyll *a*. This broadens the action spectrum over which chlorophyll *a* can fuel photosynthesis.

The Biochemistry of Photosynthesis (page 57)

1. **NADP**: Carries H_2 from the light dependent phase to the light independent reactions.
2. **Chlorophyll** molecules trap light energy and produce high energy electrons. These are used to make ATP and NADPH. The chlorophyll molecules also split water, releasing H^+ for use in the light independent reactions and liberating free O_2.
3. (a) 5C (c) 3C
   (b) 3C (X2 molecules) (d) 5C
4. (a) **Light dependent (D) phase**: Takes place in the grana (thylakoid membranes) of the chloroplast and requires light energy to proceed. The light dependent phase generates ATP and reducing power in the form of NADPH. The electrons and hydrogen ions come from the splitting of water.
   (b) **Calvin cycle**: Takes place in the stroma of the chloroplast and does not require light energy to proceed. The Calvin cycle uses ATP and NADPH from the light dependent phase, for the step-wise reduction of carbon dioxide to glucose.
5. Carbon and oxygen from carbon dioxide gas (via stomata). Hydrogen from water (via the roots and vascular system) obtained from the soil. **Note**: It has been shown through oxygen isotope studies that the free oxygen produced as a result of photosynthesis comes from water and the oxygen in the carbohydrate comes from carbon dioxide.
6. The ATP synthesis is coupled to electron transport. When the light strikes the chlorophyll molecules, high energy electrons are released by the chlorophyll molecules. The energy lost when the electrons are passed through a series of electron carriers is used to bond a phosphate to ADP to make ATP.
   Note: ATP is generated (in photosynthesis and cellular respiration) by **chemiosmosis**. As the electron carriers pick up the electrons, protons (H^+) pass into the space inside the thylakoid, creating a high concentration of protons there. The protons return across the thylakoid membrane down a concentration gradient via the enzyme complex, ATP synthetase that synthesises the ATP (also called ATP synthase or ATPase).
7. (a) **Non-cyclic (photo)phosphorylation**: Generation of ATP using light energy during photosynthesis. The electrons lost during this process are replaced by the splitting of water.

(b) The term non-cyclic **photo**phosphorylation is also (commonly) used because it indicates that the energy for the phosphorylation is coming from light.
(c) In oxidative phosphorylation, the energy for the phosphorylation comes from the oxidation of glucose (the transfer of electrons released in the oxidation is coupled to ATP synthesis).

8. In **cyclic photophosphorylation**, the electrons lost from photosystem II are replaced by those from photosystem I rather than from the splitting of water. ATP is generated in this process, but not NADPH. **Note**: In the cell, both cyclic and non-cyclic photophosphorylation operate to different degrees in order to keep the production of NADPH and ATP balanced.

Factors Affecting Photosynthesis (page 59)

1. (a) CO_2 concentration: Photosynthetic rate increases as the CO_2 concentration increases, and then levels off.
   (b) Light intensity: Photosynthetic rate increases rapidly as the light intensity increases and then levels off.
   (c) Temperature: Increased temperature increases the photosynthetic rate, but this effect is not marked at low CO_2.
2. The photosynthetic rate is determined by the rate at which CO_2 enters the leaf. When this declines because of low atmospheric levels, so does photosynthetic rate.
3. (a) By changing only one factor at a time (either temperature or CO_2 level) it is possible to assess the effects of each one separately.
   (b) CO_2 has the greatest effect of these two variables.
   (c) At low levels of CO_2, increase in temperature has little effect (the rate of CO_2 entry into the leaf is the greatest determinant of photosynthetic rate).
4. Glasshouses are controlled environments in which the levels of light, humidily, temperature, and CO_2 can be optimised to maximise photosynthetic rate. In particular, CO_2 enrichment in an environment where transpiration losses are minimised enables maximum productivity.
5. Student's own experimental design. Possible hypothesis is that temperature will increase the rate of photosynthesis within limits (H_0 being no effect of temperature). The choice of design and plant will be up to the student but an easy one to choose is to measure the rate of oxygen (air bubble) production in a submerged aquatic macrophyte such as *Elodea*. The temperature can then be easily changed by heating or cooling the water. Things the student should make reference to and explain if necessary:
   - the control and how it was set up
   - how the dependent variable (biological response) is to be measured and how many measurements will be made
   - how the independent variable (temperature) is to be varied and the range of that variation
   - how other variables are kept constant and the value of these variables (e.g. light level)
   - how many plants at each treatment level

Cellular Respiration (page 60)

1. (a) Glycolysis: cytoplasm
   (b) Krebs cycle: matrix of mitochondria
   (c) Electron transport chain: cristae (inner membrane surface) of mitochondria.
2. (a) Substrate-level phosphorylation: Formation of ATP by the transfer a phosphate group from a substrate (e.g. a phosphorylated 6C sugar) to ADP directly, with no involvement of an electron transport chain.
   (b) Oxidative phosphorylation: The process by which glucose is oxidised in a series of redox reactions and the energy released in the electron transfers is coupled to ATP synthesis.

The Biochemistry of Respiration (page 61)

1. (a) 6 carbon atoms
   (b) 3 carbon atoms (glucose split into two)
   (c) 2 carbon atoms (1 carbon lost as CO_2)
   (d) 6 carbon atoms (2-carbon acetyl added to 4 carbon)
   (e) 5 carbon atoms (1 carbon lost as CO_2)
   (f) 4 carbon atoms (1 carbon lost as CO_2)
2. (a) Glycolysis: 2 ATP
   (b) Krebs cycle: 2 ATP
   (c) Electron transport chain: 34 ATP
   (d) Total produced: 38 ATP
3. Released as carbon dioxide (CO_2) gas and breathed out through gas exchange surfaces.
4. (a) Hydrogen atoms supply energy in the form of high energy electrons. **Note**: These are passed along the respiratory chain, losing energy as they go. The energy released is used to generate ATP.
   (b) Oxygen is the final electron acceptor at the end of the respiratory chain.
5. (a) ATP is generated by **chemiosmosis**.
   (b) **In brief**: The synthesis of ATP is coupled to electron transport and movement of hydrogen ions.
   In more detail: Energy from the passage of electrons along the chain of electron carriers is used to pump protons (H^+), against their concentration gradient, into the intermembrane space, creating a high concentration of protons there. The protons return across the membrane down a concentration gradient via the enzyme complex, ATP synthetase (also called ATP synthase or ATPase), which synthesises the ATP.

Anaerobic Pathways (page 63)

1. **Aerobic respiration** requires the presence of oxygen and produces a lot of useable energy (ATP).
   Fermentation does not require oxygen and uses an alternative H^+ acceptor. There is little useable energy produced (the only ATP generated is via glycolysis)
2. (a) $2 \div 38 \times 100 = 5.3\%$ efficiency
   (b) Only a small amount of the energy of a glucose molecule is released in anaerobic respiration. The remainder stays locked up in the molecule.
3. The build up of toxic products (e.g. ethanol or lactate) inhibits further metabolic activity.

Energy Inputs and Outputs (page 65)

1. **Producers** convert energy received from an inorganic source (usually sunlight) into a form that is accessible to consumer levels. **Consumers** depend on the energy stored in the chemical bonds of biological molecules (the fats, proteins, and carbohydrates of plant and animal tissues). They too transfer energy to other levels, but energy is lost with each transfer.
2. In a grazing food web, energy moves from producers (plants) to primary consumers (herbivores) and then to secondary consumers (carnivores). This chain of energy transfer can continue several times, but eventually ends. All these consumer groups provide energy to decomposer levels. In a detrital food web, producers provide energy as dead plant material, and the primary consumers are decomposer microbes such as bacteria and fungi. Energy flows back and forth between decomposers and detritivores but herbivores and carnivores do not feature.
3. Detritivores consume (ingest) detritus and, in doing so, speed up decomposition by increasing the surface area available to decomposer bacteria. Decomposers (bacteria and fungi) also use detritus as an energy source but digestion is extracellular (enzymes are secreted in fungi or bound to the cell surface in bacteria). These enzymes break down the detritus into constituent molecules for absorption so the breakdown is more complete than is the case with detritivores.

Food Chains (page 66)

1. (a) The sun.
   (b)-(d): See diagram below.
2. (a) Each successive trophic level has less energy.
   (b) Energy is lost by respiration as it is passed from one trophic level to the next.
3. A **food chain** comprises a sequence of organisms, each of which is a source of food for the next. Food chains in ecosystems are organised according to **trophic levels**; the feeding levels that energy passes through as it proceeds through the food chain. Organisms are assigned a category according to the trophic level they occupy. Producers form the first trophic level, 1st order consumers (primary consumers) eat producers (i.e they are herbivores), 2nd order consumers (secondary consumers) eat herbivores (i.e. they are carnivores) etc. Organisms may occupy more than one trophic level depending on diet. Detritivores and decomposers obtain energy from all other trophic levels and are therefore not assigned a trophic level.
4. The eagle occupies different trophic levels at different times (depending on the prey of choice).

Constructing a Food Web (page 67)

1. Some food chain examples as below (there are others)
   (a) Algae → zooplankton → diving beetle
   (b) Algae → zooplankton → stickleback → pike
   (c) Macrophyte → great pond snail → herbivorous water beetle → stickleback → pike
   (d) Macrophyte → carp → pike
   (e) Algae → mosquito larva → *Hydra* → dragonfly larva → carp → pike
   (f) Macrophyte → herbivorous water beetle → carp → pike
   (g) Algae → zooplankton → *Asplanchna* → leech → dragonfly larva → carp → pike
   (h) Detritus → *Paramecium* → *Asplanchna* → leech → dragonfly larva → carp → pike
   (i) Detritus → great pond snail → leech → dragonfly larva → carp → pike
   (j) Detritus → *Paramecium* → mosquito larva → *Hydra* → dragonfly larva → carp → pike
2. (a) and (b) Food web: See diagram top of next page.

Energy Flow in an Ecosystem (page 69)

1. (a) 14 000 (b) 180 (c) 35 (d) 100
2. Solar energy
3. A. Photosynthesis
   B. Eating/feeding/ingestion
   C. Respiration
   D. Export (lost from this ecosystem to another)
   E. Decomposers and detritivores feeding on other decomposers and detritivores
   F. Radiation of heat to the atmosphere

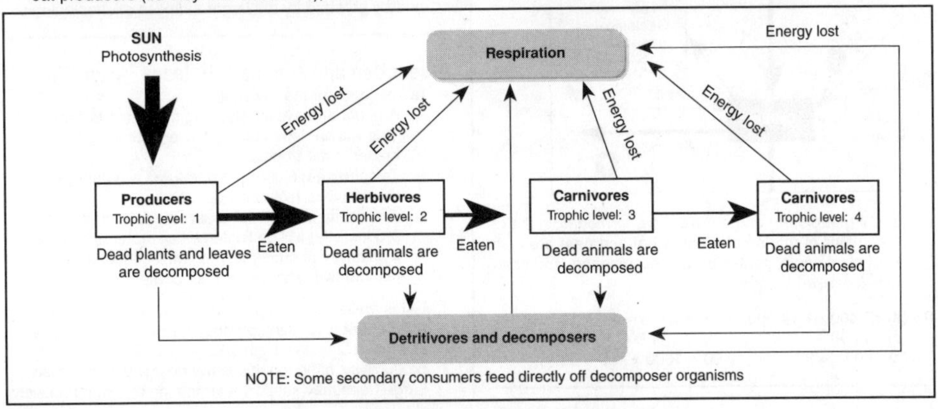

Constructing a lake foodweb:

For reasons of space, the names have been omitted from this solution but the relative positions of each organism is as presented in the workbook. Trophic levels are indicated by the letter T and the number(s) of the level(s) occupied. Note: the trophic level a species occupies will depend on the trophic position of its food items. For example, the carp occupies several different trophic levels, since it feeds on macrophytes, and on both primary and tertiary consumers. The tertiary consumers that the carp eats will also be feeding at a number of different levels, hence the complexity of food webs and the difficulty in accurately representing them in diagrams.

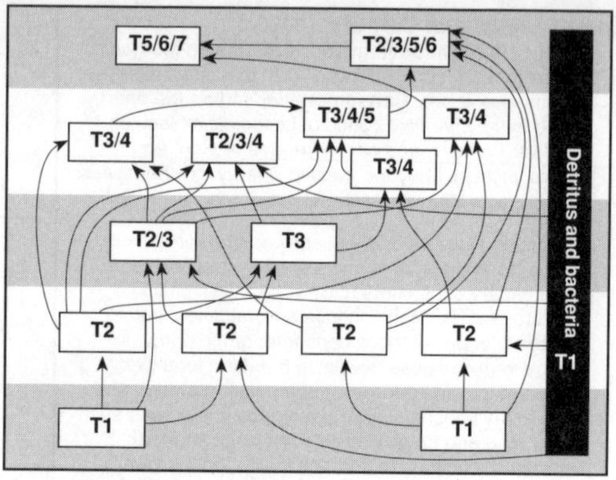

G. Excretion/egestion/death

4. (a) 1 700 000 ÷ 7 000 000 x 100 = 24.28%
   (b) It is reflected. Plants appear green because those wavelengths are not absorbed. Reflected light falls on other objects as well as back into space.

5. (a) 87 400 ÷ 1 700 000 x 100 = 5.14%
   (b) 1 700 000 - 87 400 = 1 612 600 (94.86%)
   (c) Most of the energy absorbed by the producers is **not** used in photosynthesis. This excess energy which is not fixed is lost as heat (although the heat loss component **before** the producer level is not usually shown on energy flow diagrams). **Note**: Some of the light energy absorbed through accessory pigments widens the spectrum that can drive photosynthesis. However, much of accessory pigment activity is associated with photoprotection; they absorb and dissipate excess light energy that would otherwise damage chlorophyll.

6. (a) 78 835 kJ
   (b) 78 835 ÷ 1 700 000 x 100 = 4.64%

7. (a) Decomposers and detritivores
   (b) Transport by wind or water to another ecosystem.

8. (a) Energy remains locked up in the detrital material and is not released.
   (b) Geological reservoir:

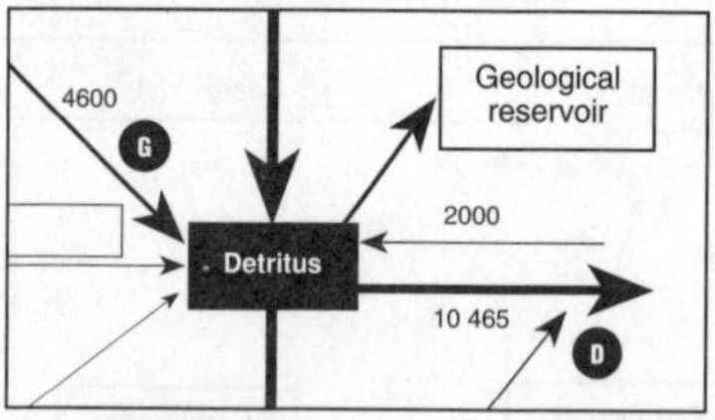

   (c) **Oil** (petroleum) and **natural gas**, formed from the remains of marine plankton. **Coal** and **peat** are both of plant origin; peat is partly decomposed, and coal is fossilised.

9. (a) 87 400 → 14 000: 14 000 ÷ 87 400 x 100 = 16%
   (b) 14 000 → 1600: 1600 ÷14 000 x 100 = 11.4%
   (c) 1600 → 90: 90 ÷ 1600 x 100 = 5.6%

Ecological Pyramids (page 71)

1. (a) Number pyramid: Numbers of individual organisms at each trophic level.
   (b) Biomass pyramid: Weight (usually dry weight) of all organisms at each trophic level.
   (c) Energy pyramid: Energy content of all organisms at each trophic level.

2. Biomass or energy pyramids usually more accurately reflect the energy available to the next trophic level than pyramids of numbers. Pyramids of numbers can be misleading because a small number of producers may represent a large amount of biomass or energy.

3. Producers include the large trees. These have a large biomass and energy content per individual.

4. (a) 8690 → 142 = 8 548 kJ = 1.6%
   (b) 142 → 12 = 130 kJ = 8.5%
   (c) Energy passed on from producers to primary consumers is less than the expected 10% because a lot of energy is diverted to the decomposers.
   (d) Decomposers
   (e) In a plankton community, turnover times (generation times of organisms) are very short and there is a lot of dead material both in the water and on the bottom. This provides a rich energy source to support a large biomass of decomposers.

5. The algae are reproducing at a high rate, but are being heavily cropped by the larger biomass of zooplankton.

Production and Trophic Efficiency (page 73)

1. (a)- (c) andy of the following:
   - Amount and availability of light for photosynthesis. This will be dependent partly on latitude and is higher in the tropics.
   - Temperature; higher temperatures are generally conducive to higher productivity.
   - Availability of water; photosynthesis (and therefore productivity) will be limited when water is scarce.
   - Availability of nutrients; nutrient limitations will limit plant growth and lower productivity.

2. LAI is an indirect measure of the capacity of the plant to intercept light, photosynthesise, and produce new plant biomass. High LAIs *may be* typical of high productivity, although this is not necessarily the case. Large trees may support a large biomass with relatively

low rates of production of new biomass. Conversely, grasslands may have high rates of production despite cropping because they are not supporting a large, static biomass. The concept is more applicable in agricultural situations where there can be marked **reductions** in the (typical) LAI for a crop, e.g. through crop damage due to pests, and this reduces the primary productivity.

3. (a) The procedure outlined only gives an estimate of NPP because you cannot easily make allowances for the plant material not collected due to consumption or death.
   (b) To express standing crop in kJ m^{-2} you would need to know the energy content of the plant material (per known mass unit measured, e.g. kg). **Note**: This could be done using a calorimeter.
   (c) To calculate GPP you need to know the energy lost in respiration, e.g. by measuring CO_2 loss at night.

4. (a)-(c) any of the following:
   - High diversity of grassland species contributing to ecosystem efficiencies (different tolerances and preferences so photosynthesis is maximised across a wide region).
   - High root production typical of herbaceous species.
   - High producer turnover because of continual cropping by herbivores so plants are always actively growing (as opposed to having a large amount of non-producing biomass like wood).
   - High rates of nutrient recycling (e.g. by termites and dung beetles) so nutrient availability is not a factor in limiting productivity.
   - Savanna occurs in equatorial or near equatorial latitudes so high light and temperature help to increase rates of plant photosynthesis.
   - Continual supplies of nutrient from the dung of primary consumers (grazing herbivores).

5. Deserts, although often high light environments, are limited by water and nutrient availability and productivities are consequently low. By contrast, intensive horticultural land is provided with plentiful water and nutrients (applied) and crops are often kept in climate controlled environments (e.g. glasshouses) to maximise temperatures and raise carbon dioxide levels. The result is very high productivities.

Increasing Agricultural Productivity (page 75)

1. The following points to be included in a discussion:
   Advantages: Increased crop growth rates and yields, production of a disease-free crop, the crop may be more aesthetically pleasing because it has no blemishes and fetch a premium price at the market, pesticides are fast acting and can control large infestations cost effectively,
   Disadvantages: Pesticides kill off all insects including beneficial ones, pesticides can accumulate in the environment and harm the local food chain (including humans), health risks to workers in the industry if pesticides are not handled correctly, pesticide resistance may develop from overuse or incorrect use, fertilisers may enter and contaminate waterways (leading to eutrophication), on a global scale fertiliser application emits greenhouse gases (N_2O) into the environment.

2. An intensive crop farm is a high energy input system. Its productivity relies on a continual supply of added nutrients, pesticides, and herbicides (energy expensive to manufacture). As it is reliant on a limited number of crop species (often a monoculture) the capacity for interspecific relationships is limited and energy transfers (from that system) end with harvest of the crop. In contrast, a natural grassland or woodland system is a low energy input system, and productivity can be variable depending on the turnover of producer biomass. Complex food webs with a large number of energy transfers (at any one trophic level) and a large number of interspecific relationships reduces energy and nutrient losses and makes the system more efficient than would otherwise be expected from a low input system.

3. (a) Antibiotics are used in intensive farming systems to prevent, control and treat disease, allowing the production of healthy animals, which in turn allows for faster animal growth.
   (b) The use of antibiotics reduces the amount of disease occurring on intensive farming systems resulting in generally healthier animals overall (given the rearing system). In some cases, the prevention of animal disease may reduce the risk of the disease spreading to humans. Frequent use of antibiotics may result in the development of bacterial resistance, and there is some concern that this resistance may spread to humans. High density farming practices are considered by some to be inhumane and only viable because the use of antibiotics to keep disease at bay.

4. Discussion could include any of the following points:

   For: Intensive farming produces a high yield (crop, meat, dairy) from a relatively small amount of land area at a cost-effective price for the consumer. As long as commodity prices are high, intensive farming is a good export earner and creates numerous jobs in related industries (e.g. fertiliser and pesticide manufacture, animal health, farm consultancy etc).

   Against: Intensive farming of livestock requires animals to be confined in small areas to the detriment of their normal behaviour and health. High animal densities increase the risk of disease (both animal and zoonotic) yet the use of antibiotics to prevent this increases the risks of spreading antibiotic resistance. Intensive farming of all sorts relies on high energy inputs, and high chemical usage can lead to excess runoff, accelerated enrichment of waterways, and pesticide bioaccumulation. As energy costs increase, high intensity systems become less economic unless stocking units are increased to levels that are detrimental to animal, crop, and environmental health. Intensive cropping also emphasises monocultures, which threatens biodiversity. In an interesting recent case (June 2009), the great hamster of Alsace is now endangered as a direct result of loss of polyculturing (barley, wheat, lucerne, cabbage) and the emphasis on growing maize (which the hamsters detest).

Options for Pest Control (page 77)

1. Top consumers are most at risk because they eat a large number of prey items from lower trophic levels (therefore larger volumes of the chemical).

2. (a) The principle of biological control is based on the

reduction of pest species to a tolerable level using natural parasites, predators, or pathogens. It is rare, and not necessarily desirable, for the pest species to be completely eliminated (if the control agent is entirely reliant on the pest, then it too will be eliminated with elimination of the pest).

(b) Precautions include the quarantine of potential biocontrol agents while their risk to the natural ecosystems is assessed. This assessment may be prolonged and involves investigating the control species biology so that predictions can be made as to how it will survive, carry out its function as a biocontrol agent, and interact with the organisms already present.

3. Persistence gives a measure of how long a chemical will stay in the environment. Highly persistent chemicals are potentially more damaging because they last long enough to become incorporated into food chains. Chemicals with a very short half life have a good chance of degrading before they are taken up by organisms.

4. The aim of IPM is not to eradicate a pest but to reduce the crop damage it causes to an economically tolerable level (a level that still makes the crop production economically viable).

5. (a) Crop monitoring (before and during the control programme) monitors the level of pest damage.
   (b) Cultivation controls combine crop management and physical means to reduce pest numbers.
   (c) If pest damage continues, biological controls, pheromone traps, and the release of sterile males are employed to control pest populations.
   (d) If pest damage remains at an unacceptable level, careful use of target-specific chemicals are used to control remaining pests.

Nutrient Cycles (page 80)

1. (a) Bacteria have the ability to make conversions to and from elements and their ionic states. This gives plants and animals access to nutrients that they would otherwise not have (i.e. increases bioavailability).
   (b) Fungi decompose organic matter, returning nutrients to the soil where plants and bacteria can access them. They are also able to convert some nutrients into more readily accessible forms.
   (c) Plants are able make their own food and, when they die, add this to the soil in the form of nutrients that can be broken down and used by bacteria and fungi. They also provide browsing animals with nutrients when they are eaten.
   (d) Animals break down materials from plants, fungi and bacteria and return then to the soil with their wastes and when they die allowing the nutrients in them to re-enter the cycle.

2. The rates of decomposition is very high in the higher temperatures of tropical forests. As a result, decaying matter is processed very quickly and very little remains in the soil. Much of the carbon and other nutrients are also locked up in biomass.

3. A macronutrient is one that is required in large amounts and often needs to be replaced on a regular basis by eating or drinking. They are often needed for growth and repair of the organism. Micronutrients (trace elements) are needed in much smaller amounts and may not need to be replaced very often. However they are often essential to the efficient operation of sensitive biochemical pathways (e.g. as enzyme cofactors).

The Nitrogen Cycle (page 81)

1. (a)-(e) any of:
   - Decomposition or decay of dead organisms, to ammonia by decomposer bacteria (ammonification).
   - Nitrification of ammonium ions to nitrite by nitrifying bacteria such as *Nitrosomonas* ($NH_4^+ \rightarrow NO_2^-$)
   - Nitrification of nitrite to nitrate by nitrifying bacteria such as *Nitrobacter* ($NO_2^- \rightarrow NO_3^-$)
   - Denitrification of nitrate to nitrogen gas by anaerobic denitrifying bacteria such as *Pseudomonas* ($NO_3^- \rightarrow N_{2(g)}$)
   - Fixation of atmospheric nitrogen to nitrate by nitrogen fixing bacteria such as *Azotobacter* and *Rhizobium* ($N_2 \rightarrow NO_3^-$)
   - Fixation of atmospheric nitrogen to ammonia by nitrogen fixing cyanobacteria ($N_2 \rightarrow NH_3$)

2. (a) Oxidation of atmospheric nitrogen by lightning.
   (b) Nitrogen fixation (by bacteria).
   (c) Production of nitrogen fertiliser through the Haber process.

3. Denitrification

4. The atmosphere.

5. Nitrate.

6. Any one of: amino acids, proteins, chlorophyll.

7. Animals ingest food (plants or other animals); they are heterotrophic.

8. Leguminous material is high in nitrogen. Ploughing it in replenishes soil nitrogen and reduces the need for additional nitrogen fertiliser when growing non-leguminous crops subsequently.

9. Human intervention in the nitrogen cycle by ((a)-(e) in any order):
   - Addition of nitrogen fertilisers to the land. This practice supplies inorganic nitrogen, as nitrate, for plant growth, but has the disadvantage that any excess nitrogen, not absorbed by plants, may enter and pollute ground water and water bodies.
   - Industrial physical-chemical fixation of nitrogen (through the Haber process) combines hydrogen and nitrogen to ammonia, which can be used to manufacture inorganic nitrogen fertilisers. This is an industrial process, which requires high temperatures and pressures and uses a large amount of energy. The effects of applied inorganic nitrogen are outlined in (a) above.
   - Genetic modification of crop plants so that they can fix nitrogen. The effect of this is to increase the range of crop plants capable of growing on nitrogen deficient soils. Potentially, this could make a beneficial contribution to soil fertility
   - Large-scale, assisted composting produces nitrogen rich organic fertiliser which has the effect of improving soil fertility and structure. This has beneficial effects in reducing the amount of inorganic nitrogen fertiliser that must be applied.

– Burning and harvesting removes nitrogen from the land and releases nitrogen oxides into the atmosphere.
– Discharge of effluent (particular animal waste) into waterways enriches water bodies and leads to localised pollution and eutrophication.
– Irrigation can accelerate loss of nitrate from the soil by increasing the rate at which nitrates are washed out of the soil into ground water.

Nitrogen Pollution (page 83)

1. (a) NO contributes to the formation of low level ozone which is a constituent of photochemical smog
(b) N_2O depletes ozone in the upper atmosphere
(c) NO_2 is a toxic inhalant. It also contributes to the formation of nitric acid in the atmosphere and therefore acid rain.
(d) $NO3^-$ is a water pollutant. It causes eutrophication, the accelerated growth of algae in waterways, and can cause severe health problems if drinking water contains significant amounts.

2. NO persists in the atmosphere both causing and being released by cyclic chemical reactions. NO reacts with oxygen to form toxic NO_2, which reacts with water to form HNO_3 (acid rain) and HNO_2. The HNO_2 decomposes, releasing NO to react again. NO will continue this cycling until it reacts with a chemical that removes it from the cycle.

3. Even after nitrogen fertilisers are not used, there is a large nitrogen load in soil and groundwater. Groundwater may take many years to move from its point of origin to its point of exit. Nitrate fertilisers that leach into groundwater now will move with this ground water and exit into waterways many years afterwards. In some cases, the lag may be up to fifty years.

4. (a) 1860: reactive N deposition in the ocean = 156.5 million tonnes. Release of unreactive nitrogen = 301 million tonnes.
1995: reactive N deposition in the ocean = 202 million tonnes. Release of unreactive nitrogen = 322 million tonnes. This is an increase of 45.5 million tonnes of reactive N deposition but an increase of only 21 million tonnes of unreactive nitrogen released Result: twice as much reactive nitrogen has been added to the ocean than has been released as unreactive nitrogen.
(b) Algal blooms are becoming more common in the oceans as nitrate levels slowly rise. Many of these blooms are from algae that contain small amounts of toxins. These can be concentrated by filter feeders such as mussels and if eaten can cause poisoning.

5. (a) Nitrates are highly soluble in water and a lot is rapidly washed away or leached from the soil and not incorporated into plant tissues. Nitrates are also broken down by bacteria and returned to the air. Some nitrates will accumulate in the soil over time but not be accessible to plants. All these factors contribute to "lost" nitrogen.
(b) Nitrogen losses could be minimised by fertiliser application at appropriate times and rates, and by sensible irrigation practices. Using slow release fertilisers in times of frequent rain also slows down the rate at which nitrates are lost into groundwater.

The Carbon Cycle (page 85)

1. Arrows can be added for the points (a)-(d) as follows:
(a) Dissolving of limestone by acid rain: Arrow from the limestone layer to atmospheric CO_2.
(b) Release of carbon from the marine food chain: Arrows (labelled **respiration**) from marine organisms to atmospheric CO_2.
(c) Mining and burning of coal: Arrow (**combustion**) from the coal seam to atmospheric carbon dioxide.
(d) Burning of plant material: Arrow (**combustion**) from the trees and/or grassland to atmospheric CO_2.

2. (a) Coal: Plant material trapped under sediment in swampy conditions millions of years ago.
(b) Oil: Marine plankton rapidly buried in fine sediment millions of years ago.
(c) Limestone (also chalk = fine limestone): Shells of molluscs, skeletons of coral and other marine organisms with skeletons of calcium carbonate piled upon seabeds and compressed.

3. Respiration (stepwise oxidation of glucose) and combustion (rapid oxidation of organic substances accompanied by heat). Both involve the release of carbon dioxide.

4. (a)-(d) in any order: Atmosphere, coal, limestone, oil and natural gas.

5. Carbon would eventually be locked up in the bodies (remains) of dead organisms. Dead matter would not rot. Possible gradual loss of CO_2 from the atmosphere.

6. (a) Photosynthesis (b) Respiration

7. (a) Dung beetles: Bury the cow manure and the larvae feed on it. Burying the dung makes it available to decomposers in the soil. The beetle larvae reprocess the dung, using it as a food source. It therefore re-enters the trophic system.
(b) Termites: Digest the cellulose in plant material, breaking it down and freeing up the carbon back into the ecosystem.
(c) Fungi: Break down dead material, utilising it as food and converting it into the fungal body. This makes it available to reenter the food chain.

8. (a) Humans deplete fossil fuel reserves through mining (they provide a source of readily available energy).
(b) The burning of fossil fuels increases the amount of carbon dioxide in the atmosphere, contributing to the rise in global temperatures. Burning also increases levels of air pollution.
(c) Minimising fossil fuels use through the use of alternative, environmentally clean sources of energy (solar energy, wind energy). Making sure that when fossil fuels are burnt, that combustion is as clean (complete) as possible, to minimise pollution.

Global Warming (page 87)

1. (a) Carbon dioxide: 30.9% increase
(b) Methane: 111.0% increase
(c) Nitrous oxide: 11.6% increase

2. Higher temperatures will result in (main points):
– Accelerated melting of the Greenland ice sheets.

- Releases of terrestrial carbon from thawing permafrost.
- Release of CH_3 from hydrates in coastal sediments.
- Expansion in ocean volume. Extra water (previously locked up in glaciers) will add to this increase.
- Arctic melt season begins earlier and ends later.
- Many Arctic species (e.g. polar bears) are at risk, especially those that inhabit the low lying areas near the sea and those that rely on cold weather conditions. Glaciers and ice sheets provide floating oases for wildlife (e.g. for rest when moving between bergs) and disappearing habitat is already forcing species such as polar bears and seals to make longer, riskier swims.
- Reductions in sea ice reduce habitat for marine zooplankton (e.g. amphipods) and shifts species assemblages of phytoplankton. Both of these consequences alter the dynamics and resilience of marine food chains.
- Tundra ecosystems will also be adversely affected as permafrost loses depth and species from all trophic levels are lost or replaced.
- Positive feedback loops are inherent in all these changes as multiple processes accelerate ice loss.

3. Increased levels of carbon dioxide, methane, and nitrous oxides act as additional blankets around the Earth, allowing the sun's energy to reach the Earth's surface, but preventing the heat escaping. This means that the Earth slowly heats up.

4. Any one of:
   - Most national governments have signed and ratified the Kyoto Protocol aimed at combating greenhouse gas emissions.
   - Measures are in place to reduce or reverse future warming or to adapt to its expected consequences (mitigation or adaptation). Examples include reducing dependence on fossil fuels and long term planning to prepare for sea level rise and more severe weather events etc.)
   - Carbon credit schemes provide a tradable permit scheme to create a market for reducing greenhouse emissions by giving a monetary value to the cost of polluting the air.

Effects of Global Warming (page 89)

1. Global warming will result in an increased frequency of weather extremes (floods, droughts etc) and a loss of land as coastal areas are inundated. Erosion rates may also increase as a result. Glacial retreats will reduce water supplies and snow lines will increase in altitude. Climate changes may shift the governing physical environment in certain regions (and consequently cause a shift in predominant vegetation). Ocean pH will also fall as a result of CO_2 absorption (again, with consequent changes in biotic communities).

2. (a) In general, crop growing ranges may shrink, expand, or shift. Crop plants may be affected more by higher night temperatures than by higher daytime temperatures. High night temperatures affect the ability of some crop plants such as rice to set seed and fruit. This will cause a reduction in the harvest, and a decrease in the amount of seed available for subsequent plantings.
   (b) Farmers may adjust by planting different crops in some areas, e.g. crops that are able to grow and set seed in the higher temperatures. New strains of crop plants may be able to be developed for the higher temperatures.

3. Fossil evidence from studies of browse damage show a significant increase in the number of damaged leaves coincident with temperature peaks just under 56 mya. If insect populations respond similarly to future temperature increases, crop damage could increase.

4. (a) Migratory birds in the northern hemisphere are now not travelling as far south during the winter months (as higher latitudes become more hospitable) and they are making their migrations north up to two weeks earlier than usual.
   (b) Migratory birds may arrive at feeding grounds before the main food supply is ready. Plants with daylength-dependent flowering may not yet be flowering and, as a consequence, insects (and seeds and fruits) may not be in the abundance required to feed the migrants. In addition, the distribution of food resources may remain the same, but the birds are not migrating as far south and may be disconnected from their winter food supplies.

5. As air temperatures rise, so too does the snow line in alpine areas. Animals living on or above the snow line will be forced into smaller areas. If they are unable to move to higher latitudes where the snow line is lower, it is inevitable that they will become extinct in their native ranges as they run out of food and space.

Primary Succession (page 92)

1. Glacial retreat, exposed slip, new volcanic island.

2. (a) Lichens and bryophytes (mosses and liverworts), as well as some hardy annual herb species, are often the first to colonise bare ground.
   (b) Chemically and physically erode the rock (producing the beginnings of a soil) and add nutrients by decay.

3. Climax communities tend to have greater biodiversity and a more complex trophic structure than early successional communities. A greater diversity of community interactions buffers the system against disturbances because there are many more organisms with different ecological roles able to compensate for losses from the system.

Secondary Succession (page 93)

1. **Primary succession** refers to the colonisation of regions where there is no preexisting community (e.g. rocky slope, exposed slip, new volcanic island). Changes in the community occur in stages until a climax community is reached. **Secondary succession** follows the interruption of an established climax community (e.g. logging, pasture reverting to bush).

2. Secondary succession proceeds more rapidly than is the case with primary succession because although the land is cleared, there is minimal or no loss of soil or seed stores. Many plants may still be able to grow despite the disturbance and the climax community will reestablish faster because nutrients are already available and seeds already laid down.

3. Events that result in secondary succession include forest fires, minor landslides, or storm or cyclonic

damage, the fall of a canopy tree, flooding, or human induced land clearance.

4. (a) Selective logging causes gaps in the canopy with the loss of the large trees. This results in a chance for new seedlings to gain more light and grow up. These seedlings may be the same or different from the species that was/were removed. Forest composition is changed by becoming temporarily more open, with a loss of the dominant large trees.
   (b) Selective logging is considered (by some) to be preferable to clear felling because there is still a favourable environment in which seedlings can mature. Canopy gaps are created naturally by windfalls; selective logging is said to mimic this, so the gaps created *may* be beneficial for forest diversity and regeneration. Clear felling, in contrast, removes all forest from the area leaving an environment unfavourable for the regeneration of existing forest species but favourable for weeds. **Note**: Some conservationists oppose this view as selective logging may still do lasting damage to forest structure and diversity.

5. (a) A **deflected succession** refers to a succession that is deflected from its natural course by human intervention. A climax community (a plagioclimax) develops that is different from the one that would have developed if the intervention had not occurred.
   (b) Many human-modified landscapes (e.g. agricultural lands, grasslands, woodlands) are managed (by burning, grazing, mowing) with the express purpose of preventing the establishment of a natural climax community. These communities are quite distinct from those that would naturally develop if the land were left alone.

Wetland Succession (page 95)

1. (a) Low evaporation rates (b) High rainfall

2. Both these conditions are found at high latitudes and/or high altitudes.

3. Land drainage threatens bog ecosystems because it dries out the soil and allows acid intolerant species to invade and compete with the natural bog species.

4. *Sphagnum* lowers the pH of the surrounding soil and hampers the establishment of the acid intolerant species typical of swamps and fens. Acid tolerant (bog) species can then become established.

Conservation and Succession (page 96)

1. In areas where forest fires are common the ultimate climax community may never arise as fire removes old growth trees. Only young or fast growing trees are able to survive. Periodic floods may have the same effect if vegetation is removed on a regular basis.

2. Some plants and animals are characteristic of certain habitats, e.g. grassland or moorland. These particular habitats would be lost if allowed to follow a normal succession to forest or woodland. To maintain them, along with their characteristic flora and fauna, the earlier successional stage must be maintained. order to maintain the population the community must not be allowed to progress to the next stage of succession

3. If properly managed, a deflected climax will preserve the integrity of a certain suite of plants and animals. It protects habitat-dependent species that might otherwise be threatened with loss, and preserves the diversity of ecosystem type within a region.

Alleles (page 99)

1. (a) Heterozygous: Each of the homologous chromosomes contains a **different** allele for the gene (one dominant and one recessive).
   (b) Homozygous dominant: Each of the homologous chromosomes contains an identical dominant allele.
   (c) Homozygous recessive: Each of the homologous chromosomes contains an identical recessive allele.

2. (a) **Aa** (b) **AA** (c) **aa**

3. Each chromosome of a **homologous pair** comes from a different parent: one of maternal origin, one of paternal origin (they originated from the egg and the sperm that formed the zygote). They contain the same sequence of genes for the same traits, but the versions of the genes (alleles) on each chromosome may differ.

4. **Alleles** are different versions of the same gene that code for the same trait. Different alleles provide phenotypic variation for the expression of a gene. There are often two alleles for a gene, one dominant and one recessive. In this case, the dominant allele will be expressed in the phenotype. Sometimes alleles for a gene can be equally dominant, in which case, both alleles will be expressed in the phenotype. Where three or more alleles for a gene exist (multiple alleles), there is more phenotypic variation in the population (for that trait) than would be the case with just two alleles.

Genes, Inheritance, and Selection (page 100)

1. Sexual reproduction, through independent assortment and random combination of gametes at fertilisation, shuffles alleles into new combinations. The new allele combinations provide variation, the raw material on which natural selection acts. Selection acts on the phenotype (being the result of genotype and environment). Selection acts for or against particular allele combinations, enhancing or reducing the representation of these in the next generation. Selection therefore sorts the variability in a gene pool and establishes adaptive genotypes.

2. Mutations (changes in the DNA) as a result of transcription errors or mutagens provide new alleles in asexual organisms.

3. Each individual has an effectively unique combination of alleles. Allele combinations in related individuals are more similar than between them and more distantly related individuals. Each individual is subjected to selection pressures that will affect its ability to survive and reproduce. In this way, the individual's allele combination is tested, with the better suited being able to produce more surviving offspring.

Monohybrid Cross (page 101)

	Genotype	Phenotype
Cross 2	50% BB 50% Bb	100% black
Cross 3	25% BB 50% Bb 25% bb	75% black 25% white

Cross 4	100% BB	100% black
Cross 5	50% Bb 50% bb	50% black 50% white
Cross 6	100% bb	100% white

The Test Cross (page 102)

1. To perform the test cross here you would have to cross the male with a female (brown eye, ebony body) homozygous recessive for both genes (bbee).
   Extra information:
   Depending on the male's genotype the outcomes of the test cross would produce offspring that were:
   - All wild type (brown body red eye)
   - Half wild type, and half red eye, ebony body
   - Half wild type, and half brown eye, brown body
   - 25% wild type, 25% red eye ebony, 25% brown eye, brown body, and 25% brown eye, ebony.

   Students may choose to present this information in Punnett squares.

Male gametes (columns); Female gametes (rows)

	BE
eb	BbEe
	red eye, brown body

	BE	Be
eb	BbEe	Bbee
	red eye, brown body	red eye, ebony body

	BE	bE
eb	BbEe	bbEe
	red eye, brown body	brown eye, brown body

	BE	Be	bE	be
eb	BbEe	Bbee	bbEe	bbee
	red eye, brown body	red eye, ebony body	brown eye, brown body	brown eye, ebony body

2. A wild type male (brown or normal body and red eyes) could have one of four genotypes:
   BEBE, BEbE, BEBe, or BEbe
3. (a) 50% are wild type and 50% are red eye, ebony so the male must BEBe.
   (b) This is the only genotype that produces this ratio of phenotypes in the offspring (as per the second Punnett square above)

Dominance of Alleles (page 103)

1. (a) **Incomplete dominance**: Neither allele is dominant (neither can mask the other).
   (b) **Codominance**: Two or more alleles are dominant over any recessive alleles; both are fully expressed.
2. (a) Incomplete dominance: Heterozygote's phenotype is intermediate between homozygous parents.
   (b) Codominance: Heterozygotes have a phenotype that is different from either homozygous parent.
3. Ratio: **1 : 2 : 1** (1 red : 2 roan : 1 white).

Male gametes (columns); Female gametes (rows)

	C^R	C^W
C^R	C^RC^R	C^RC^W
C^W	C^RC^W	C^WC^W

4. Parents: white and pink. Will produce 50% pink and 50% white offspring.

Male gametes (columns); Female gametes (rows)

	C^W	C^W
C^R	C^RC^W	C^RC^W
C^W	C^WC^W	C^WC^W

5. (a) Diagram labels:

	White bull	**Roan cow**
Parent genotype:	C^WC^W	C^RC^W
Gametes:	C^W, C^W	C^R, C^W
Calf genotypes:	C^RC^W, C^WC^W, C^RC^W, C^WC^W	
Phenotypes:	roan, white, roan, white	

   (b) Phenotype ratio: 50% roan, 50% white (1:1)
   (c) By choosing only the roan calves (male and female) to breed from. Initial offspring from roan parents should include all phenotypes: white, roan and red. By selecting just the red offspring from this generation it would be possible to breed a pure herd of red cattle. The unwanted phenotypes must be prevented from breeding (e.g. by castration).

6. (a) Diagram labels:

	Unknown bull	**Roan cow**
Parent Genotype:	C^RC^R	C^RC^W
Gametes:	C^R,C^R	C^R,C^W
Calf Genotypes:	C^RC^R, C^RC^W, C^RC^R, C^RC^W	
Phenotypes:	red, roan, red, roan	

   (b) Unknown bull: **red**

7. (a) Diagram labels:

	Pink	**Red**
Parent Genotype:	C^RC^W	C^RC^R
Gametes:	C^R, C^W	C^R, C^R
Offspring:	C^RC^R, C^RC^R, C^RC^W, C^RC^W	
Phenotypes:	red, red, pink, pink	

   (b) Phenotype ratio: **50% red, 50% pink**

Multiple Alleles in Blood Groups (page 105)

Note: In this activity, any reference to the I alleles has been removed on the advice of researchers involved in the latest work in this area. References to the I gene are now considered to be incorrect and misleading.

1. Blood group table:

Blood group **B**	BB, BO
Blood group **AB**	AB

2.

Cross 2	**Group O**	**Group O**
Gametes:	O, O	O, O
Children's genotypes:	OO, OO	OO, OO
Blood groups:	O, O	O, O

Cross 3	Group AB	Group A
Gametes:	A, B	A, O
Children's genotypes:	AA, AO	BA, BO
Blood groups:	A, A	AB, B

Cross 4	Group A	Group B
Gametes:	A, A	B, O
Children's genotypes:	AB, AO	AB, AO
Blood groups:	AB, A	AB, A

Cross 5	Group A	Group O
Gametes:	A, O	O, O
Children's genotypes:	AO, AO	OO, OO
Blood groups:	A, A	O, O

Cross 6	Group B	Group O
Gametes:	B, O	O, O
Children's genotypes:	BO, BO	OO, OO
Blood groups:	B, B	O, O

Note: It is possible to have the answers arranged differently, depending on which gamete circle each symbol of a gene is placed, . There are of course many more crossover combinations possible.

3. (a)

Parent genotype:	AO	OO
Gametes:	A, O	O, O
Children's genotypes:	AO, AO	OO, OO
Blood groups:	A, A	O, O

(b) 50%
(c) 50%
(d) 0%

4. (a) Possible parent genotypes: Mother assumed to be heterozygous to get maximum variation in gametes (homozygous would also work).

Phenotypes	**Group A**	**Group O**
Genotypes:	AO	OO
Gametes:	A, O	O, O

Child's genotype would have to be AO or OO

(b) Therefore the only possible offspring from this couple would have been children with group **A** or group **O**. The man making the claim could not have been the father of the child.

5. (a) **A** or **B** (b) **AB, A, B** or **O**

Sex Linkage (page 107)

1.

Parent genotype:	X_oX_o	X_OY
Gametes:	X_o, X_o	X_O, Y
Kitten genotypes:	X_oX_O, X_oY	X_oX_O, X_oY
	Genotypes	**Phenotypes**
Male kittens:	X_oY	Black
Female kittens:	X_oX_O	Tortoiseshell

2.

Parent genotype:	X_oX_O	X_OY
Gametes:	X_o, X_O	X_O, Y
Kitten genotypes:	X_OX_O, X_oX_O	X_oY, X_OY
Phenotypes:	Orange female, Tortoise female	Black male, Orange male

(a) Father's genotype: X_OY
(b) Father's phenotype: Orange

3.

Parent genotype:	X_oX_o	X_OY
Gametes:	X_o, X_o	X_O, Y
Kitten genotypes:	X_oX_O, X_oY	X_oX_O, X_oY
Phenotypes:	Tortoise female, Black male	Tortoise female, Black male

(a) Father's genotype: X_OY
(b) Father's phenotype: Orange
(c) Yes, the same male could have fathered both litters.

4.

Parent:	Normal wife	Affected husband
Parent genotype:	XX	X_RY
Gametes:	X, X	X_R, Y
Child genotypes:	X_RX, XY	X_RX, XY
Phenotypes:	Affected girl, Normal boy	Affected girl, Normal boy

(a) Probability of having affected children = 50% or 0.5
(b) Probability of having an affected girl = 50% or 0.5
However, all girls born will be affected = 100%
(c) Probability of having an affected boy = 0% or none

5.

Parent:	Affected wife	Normal husband
Parent genotype:	X_RX	XY
Gametes:	X_R, X	X, Y
Child genotypes:	X_RX, X_RY	XX, XY
Phenotypes:	Affected girl, Affected boy	Normal girl, Normal boy

Note: Because the wife had a normal father, she must be heterozygous since her father was able to donate only an X-chromosome with the normal condition.

(a) Probability of having affected children = 50% or 0.5
(b) Probability of having an affected girl = 25% or 0.25
However, half of all girls born may be affected
(c) Probability of having an affected boy = 25% or 0.25
However, half of all boys born may be affected.

Background information for question 6: Sex linkage refers to the location of genes on one or other of the sex chromosomes (usually the X chromosome; but a few are carried on the Y). Such genes produce an inheritance pattern which is different from that shown by autosomes:

- Reciprocal crosses produce different results (unlike autosomal genes that produce the same results).
- Males carry only one allele of each gene.
- Dominance operates in females only.
- A 'cross-cross' inheritance pattern is produced: father to daughter to grandson, etc.

6. **Sex linkage** (in humans, this usually means X-linkage) is involved in a number of genetic disorders (see below). X-linked disorders are commonly seen only in males (the heterogametic sex), because they have only one locus for the gene and must express the trait. If the sex linked trait is due to a recessive allele, females will express the phenotype only when homozygous recessive. It is possible for females to inherit a double dose of the recessive allele (e.g. a colour blind daughter can be born to a colour blind father and mother who is a carrier), but this is much less likely than in males because sex linked traits are relatively uncommon. Over a hundred X-linked genes are known, including those that control:
   - Blood clotting: A recessive allele for this gene causes haemophilia. It affects about 0.01% of males but is almost unheard of in females.
   - Normal colour vision: A recessive allele causes red-green colour blindness affecting 8% of males but only 0.7% of females.
   - Antidiuretic hormone production: A version of this gene causes some forms of diabetes insipidus.
   - Muscle development: A rare recessive allele causes Duchene muscular dystrophy.

Gene Pools and Evolution (page 109)

1. & 2. **Note**: Do not include aa about to enter Deme 1, but do include Aa about to leave Deme 1. For the purpose of the exercise, assume that the individual with the mutation **A'A** in Deme 1 is a normal **AA** combination.

Deme 1: 22 beetles Deme 2: 19 beetles

Deme 1		Number counted	%
Allele types	*A*	26	59.1
	a	18	40.9
Allele combinations	*AA*	8	36.4
	Aa	10	45.4
	aa	4	18.2

Deme 2		Number counted	%
Allele types	*A*	13	34.2
	a	25	65.8
Allele combinations	*AA*	1	5.3
	Aa	11	57.9
	aa	7	36.8

3. (a) **Population size**: Large population acts as a 'buffer' for random, directional changes in allele frequencies. A small population can exhibit changes in allele frequencies because of random loss of alleles (failure of an individual to contribute young to the next generation).
   (b) **Mate selection**: Random mating occurs in many animals and most plants. With 'mate selection', there is no random meeting of gametes, and certain combinations come together at a higher frequency than would occur by chance alone. This will alter the frequency of alleles in subsequent generations.
   (c) **Gene flow between populations**: Immigration (incoming) and emigration (outgoing) has the effect of adding or taking away alleles from a population that can change allele frequencies. In some cases, two-way movements may cancel, with no net effect.
   (d) **Mutations**: A source of new alleles. Most are harmful, confer poor fitness, and will be lost from the gene pool over a few generations. Some may be neutral, conferring no advantage over organisms with different alleles. Occasionally, mutations may confer greater fitness and will increase in frequency at the expense of other alleles.
   (e) **Natural selection**: Selection pressures will affect some allele types more than others, causing allele frequencies to change with each generation.
4. (a) Increase genetic variation: Gene flow (migration), large population size, mutation.
   (b) Decrease genetic variation: Natural selection, non-random mating (mate selection), genetic drift.

Hardy-Weinberg Calculations (page 111)

The answers to the panels provided in the workbook are shown below as working. Alternatively, these calculations are quickly done using a spreadsheet.

1. **Working**: q= 0.1, p= 0.9, q^2 = 0.01, p^2 = 0.81, 2pq=0.18
   Proportion of black offspring = 2pq + p^2 x 100% = 99%;
   Proportion of grey offspring = q^2 x 100% = 1%
2. **Working**: q= 0.3, p= 0.7, q^2 = 0.09, p^2 = 0.49, 2pq=0.42
   (a) Frequency of tall (dominant) gene (allele): 70%
   (b) 42% heterozygous; 42% of 400 = **168**
3. **Working**: q= 0.6, p= 0.4, q^2 = 0.36, p^2 = 0.16, 2pq=0.48
   (a) 40% dominant allele
   (b) 48% heterozygous; 48% of 1000 = **480**
4. **Working**: q= 0.2, p= 0.8, q^2 = 0.04, p^2 = 0.64, 2pq=0.32
   (a) 32% heterozygous (carriers)
   (b) 80% dominant allele
5. **Working**: q= 0.5, p= 0.5, q^2 = 0.25, p^2 = 0.25, 2pq= 0.5
   Proportion of population that becomes white = 25%
6. **Working**: q= 0.8, p= 0.2, q^2= 0.64, p^2= 0.04, 2pq= 0.32
   (a) 80% (c) 36% (e) 96%
   (b) 32% (d) 4%
7. **Working**: q= 0.1, p= 0.9, q^2= 0.01, p^2= 0.81, 2pq= 0.18
   Proportion of people expected to be albino (i.e. proportion that are homozygous recessive) = 1%

Analysis of a Squirrel Gene Pool (page 113)

1. Graph of population changes:

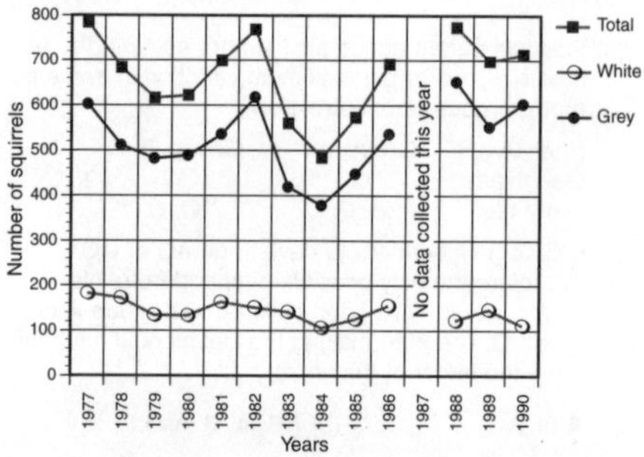

   (a) 784 to 484 = 61% fluctuation
   (b) Total population numbers exhibit an oscillation with a period of 5-6 years (2 cycles). Fluctuations occur in both normal grey and albino populations.

2. Graph of genotype changes:

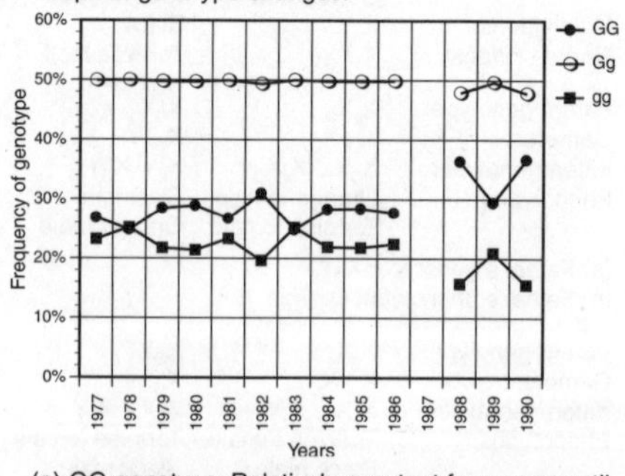

   (a) GG genotype: Relatively constant frequency until

the last 3-4 years which exhibit an increase. Could also argue that there is an increase over the total sampling period.

(b) Gg genotype: Uniform frequency.

(c) gg genotype: Relatively constant frequency until the last 3-4 years which exhibit a decline. One could also argue for a decrease over the total period.

3. Graph of allele changes:

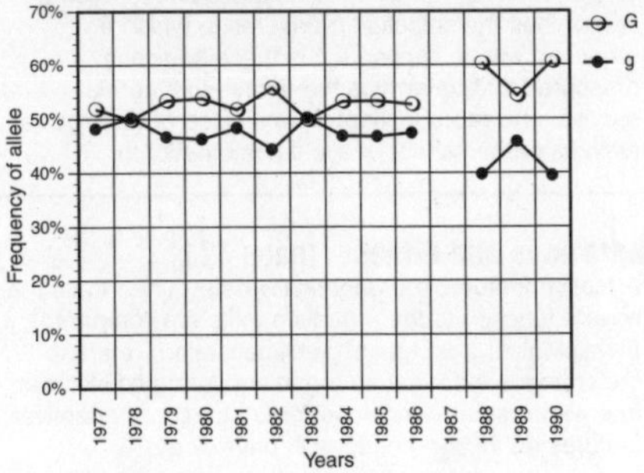

(a) Frequency of G: Increases in the last 3-4 years.

(b) Frequency of g: Decreases in the last 3-4 years.

4. (a) The frequency of alleles graph (to a lesser extent the frequency of genotypes graph)

(b) Changes in allele frequencies in a population provide the best indication of significant evolutionary changes occurring. These cannot be deduced simply from changes in numbers or genotypes.

5. There are at least two possible causes (any one of):
   - Genetic drift in a relatively small population, i.e. there are random changes in allele frequencies as a result of small population size.
   - Natural selection against albinos. Albinism represents a selective disadvantage in terms of survival and reproduction (albinos are more vulnerable to predators because of greater visibility and have lower fitness generally).

Natural Selection (page 115)

1. Selection always operates in the environment of the time. For example, in a time of drought, selection might favour two phenotypic extremes (disruptive) but that pressure may be very different in a more favourable environment. Selection pressures are not static; they shift constantly with shifts in the environment.

2. Stable environments favour the most common phenotypes. Environmental instability provides a chance that extreme phenotypes might be advantageous, but in a stable environment, this is unlikely to happen. Predictability encourages a reduction in phenotypic variability because this is no disadvantage when the environment is largely static.

3. (a) Drought favoured birds with beak sizes at two extremes of the range, since these birds could exploit the small and the large seed sizes.

(b) Continuation of the drought could lead to further divergence in beak size.

(c) The selection pressures favouring a bimodal distribution in beak size would be reduced and medium sized beaks would become relatively more common (i.e. there would be a shift from disruptive to stabilising selection).

4. Women have a higher requirement than males for calcium during pregnancy and lactation, and calcium absorption is dependent on vitamin D. The selection pressure on females for lighter skins (to maximise UV absorption/vitamin D synthesis) is therefore greater than for males.

5. The Inuit people have such abundant vitamin D in their diet that the selection pressure for lighter skin (for UV absorption and vitamin D synthesis) is reduced and their skin can be darker.

6. People of African origin living in northern UK must take vitamin D supplements to compensate for their lack of UV absorption and to prevent them getting rickets or (the adult equivalent) osteomalacia.

Heterozygous Advantage (page 117)

1. People who are heterozygous for the sickle cell gene are somewhat affected by sickle cell anaemia but have considerable resistance to malaria which is widespread in the region. This **heterozygous advantage** maintains the mutant allele at a relatively stable frequency in the population despite its deleterious effects. The stable coexistence of both the sickle cell allele and the normal allele exemplifies a **balanced polymorphism**.

Selection for Human Birth Weight (page 118)

Histogram as below. Sample data if required follow.

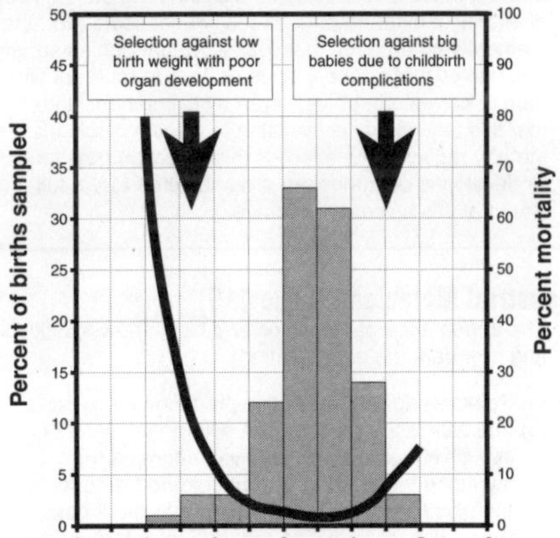

Note: For the construction of weight classes, it is necessary to have a range of weight categories that do not overlap. The data collected should be sorted into weight classes of: 0.0-0.49, 0.50-0.99, 1.0-1.49, 1.5-1.99, etc.

SAMPLE DATA: Use these data if students are unable to collect from local sources.

3.740	3.830	3.530	3.095	3.630
1.560	3.910	4.180	3.570	2.660
3.150	3.400	3.380	2.660	3.375

3.840	3.630	3.810	2.640	3.955
2.980	3.350	3.780	3.260	4.510
3.800	4.170	4.400	3.770	3.400
3.825	3.130	3.400	3.260	4.100
3.220	3.135	3.090	3.830	3.970
3.840	4.710	4.050	4.560	3.350
3.380	3.690	1.495	3.260	3.430
3.510	3.230	3.570	3.620	3.260
3.315	3.230	3.790	2.620	3.030
3.350	3.970	3.915	2.040	4.050
3.105	3.790	3.060	2.770	3.400
1.950	3.800	2.390	2.860	4.110
1.970	3.800	4.490	2.640	3.550
4.050	4.220	2.860	4.060	3.740
4.082	3.000	3.230	2.800	4.050
4.300	3.030	3.160	3.300	2.350
3.970	2.980	3.550	3.070	2.715

1. Approximating a statistically normal distribution curve or bell-shaped curve (there may be a skew to the left).
2. 3.5 kg (taken from the table: only 2% mortality).
3. Good correlation. Lowest frequencies of surviving birth weights correspond to birth weights of highest mortality.
4. There are two selection pressures operating at opposite ends of the birth weight range. Premature babies have reduced survival capacity because their body systems are not fully developed. Large babies present problems with delivery, as the birth canal can only accommodate babies up to a certain size. Very large babies can occur when mothers have or develop diabetes during pregnancy. Before adequate medical intervention was developed, very large babies often lead to the death of both mother and baby.
5. Modern medical technologies are ensuring the survival of infants at extreme ends of the weight scale (and the mothers who produce them). Low weight babies survive and babies that are very large or born to mothers with narrow pelves can be delivered by Caesarian. Note that this technology is available to wealthy societies thereby reducing the effect of this selection pressure. Undeveloped countries are still subjected to the full extent of this selection pressure.

Industrial Melanism (page 119)

1. The appearance of the wings and body (how speckled and how dark the pigmentation).
2. (a) Selective agent is selective predation by birds.
   (b) The selection pressure (the differential effect of selective predation on survival) changed from favouring the survival of light coloured morphs in the unpolluted environments prior to the Industrial Revolution, to favouring the dark morph (over the light morph) during the Industrial Revolution (when there was a lot of soot pollution). In more recent times, with air quality improving, the survival of the light coloured morphs has once again improved.
3. There was a high frequency of the melanic form in and around industrial regions; the grey mottled form was more prevalent in non-industrial regions.
4. (a) Summer smoke from 75 to 15 μgm^{-3} (80% drop). Winter SO_2 from 140 to 15 μgm^{-3} (90% drop).
   (b) Melanic form frequency dropped from 95% to 50%.
5. The selection pressure (resulting from bird predation) is disruptive, affecting the two morphs differently in different environments.
6. **Natural** selection occurs without human intervention, in response to normal environmental changes. In contrast, **artificial** selection is directed specifically by humans, usually towards a specific phenotypic result.
7. The environment (including the biotic environment) determines the selection pressures to which an organism will be exposed. It is these selection pressures that determine the fitness (differential survival and reproduction) or otherwise of an organism (with its particular set of allele combinations).

Adaptations and Fitness (page 121)

1. Adaptive features are genetically determined traits that have a function to the organism in its environment. Physiological 'adaptation' (acclimatisation) refers to the changes made by an organism during its lifetime to environmental conditions (note that some adaptive features do involve changes in physiology).
2. Shorter extremities are associated with colder climates, whereas elongated extremities are associated with warmer climates. The differences are associated with heat conservation (shorter limbs/ears lose less heat to the environment).
3. Large body sizes conserve more heat and have more heat producing mass relative to the surface area over which heat is lost.

Isolation and Species Formation (page 122)

1. Isolating mechanisms protect the gene pool from the diluting and potentially adverse effects of introduced genes. Species are finely tuned to their niche; foreign genes will usually reduce fitness.
2. (a) Geographical isolation physically separates populations (and gene pools) but, if reintroduced, the two populations could potentially interbreed, i.e. reproductive isolation may not have occurred.
   (b) Geographical isolation enables populations to diverge in response to different selection pressures and (potentially) develop reproductive isolating mechanisms. Reproductive isolation won't generally occur in a populations in which there is gene flow (unless by special events such as polyploidy).
3. Geographical isolation physically separates populations (gene pools) so there is no gene flow between them. Ecological isolation arises as a result of different preferences in habitat or behaviour even though the populations occupy the same geographical area.

Reproductive Isolation (page 123)

1. (a) Postzygotic: hybrid breakdown
   (b) Prezygotic: structural
   (c) Prezygotic: temporal
   (d) Postzygotic: hybrid inviability
2. They are a secondary backup if the first isolating mechanism fails. The majority of species do not interbreed because of prezygotic mechanisms. Postzygotic mechanisms are generally rarer events.

Allopatric Speciation (page 125)

1. Interspecific competition, intraspecific competition (this is the strongest). New habitat becomes available (loss of geographical barrier).

2. (a) Plants move by dispersal of their seeds (water borne, carried vast distance by winds, animals carry them in their fur/feathers or in their gut to be deposited with their faeces).
   (b) Gene flow between the parent population and dispersing populations is regular. Gene flow refers to the movement of genes, via gametes, from one population to another.

3. Orogeny or plate tectonics (continental drift).

4. Ice ages, glacials, or interglacials.

5. Mountains form. Rivers form or change course. Deserts. Isthmus or land bridge forms (land separating two seas, e.g. Central America). Ice sheets advance. Sea or ocean develops (due to continental drift).

6. Physical (or geographical) barriers prevent the movement of organisms between populations and thereby restrict or prevent gene flow between separated populations. Once this happens, populations may diverge genetically on either side of the physical barrier.

7. (a) Selection pressures on gene pools (any four of): Various climatic factors (e.g. temperature, pH, salinity, wind exposure), competition, predation, disease and parasitism, quality of the food resource.
   (b) Some individuals will have allele combinations (and therefore a phenotype) that better suits the unique set of selection pressures at a given location. Over a period of time (generations) certain alleles for a gene will become more common in the gene pool, at the expense of other less suited alleles.

8. Reproductive isolating mechanisms:
   (see pages 122-124 of the workbook for full descriptions).
   (a) **Prezygotic** (prevent fertilisation from taking place): Spatial, ecological, temporal, behavioural, structural, gamete mortality.
   (b) **Postzygotic** (fertilisation occurs, but the result is unsuccessful, to varying degrees): Zygote mortality, reduced fertility, hybrid breakdown.

9. **Allopatry** refers to the situation where populations within the species have separate areas of geographical range. **Sympatry** refers to the situation where populations within the species inhabit the same or overlapping geographical areas.

Detecting Changing States (page 130)

1. Appropriate responses aid survival and enable effective interpretation about the changing state of the environment. For example, pain withdrawal response prevents a burned hand, running away from a snarling dog avoids attack etc.

2. (a) and (b) any from the examples provided (or others). Answers provided as stimulus (receptor):
   (a) External stimuli and their receptors: Light (photoreceptor cells); gravity (hair cells/vestibule of the inner ear); sound/vibration (hair cells in the cochlea of the inner ear); airborne chemicals (olfactory receptors in the nose); dissolved chemicals (taste buds); external pressure (dermal pressure receptors, e.g. Pacinian corpuscle, Meissner's corpuscles); pain (nerve endings in the dermis); temperature (nerve endings in the skin).
   (b) Internal stimuli and their receptors: Blood pH/ carbon dioxide level (chemoreceptors in blood vessels); blood pressure (baroreceptors); stretch (proprioreceptors, e.g. muscle spindle).

Taxes and Kineses (page 131)

1. A **kinesis** describes movement of a cell or organism in which the *rate* of movement depends upon the intensity (rather than direction) of the stimulus. An example is the increased activity of body lice when temperature increases over 30°C. In contrast, a **taxis** is a *directional* movement of a cell or organism in response to an external stimulus. An example is the negative phototaxis of maggots.

2. Such simple behaviours allow an animal to continue making random orientation responses until it is in an environment favourable to its survival (e.g. body lice must reach an appropriate host, as indicated by the surface skin temperature). Once positioned, the behaviour will cease until environmental conditions change once again.

3. (a) Gravi – Gravity
   (b) Hydro – Water/moisture/humidity
   (c) Thigmo – Touch
   (d) Photo – Light
   (e) Chemo – Chemical
   (f) Thermo – Heat

4. (a) Snails: negative gravitaxis.
   (b) Moth: positive chemotaxis.
   (c) Louse: kinesis in response to temperature.
   (d) Lobster: positive thigmotaxis.
   (e) Mosquitoes: positive thermotaxis.
   (f) Maggots: negative phototaxis.

5. 30°C

Plant Responses (page 132)

1. Light (including the light/dark cycle), gravity, temperature, touch, chemicals.

2. Appropriate responses to environmental stimuli enable the plant to synchronise its daily cycles and seasonally important events, such as germination, with environmental cues. Appropriate responses enhance survival in different environments.

Tropisms and Growth Responses (page 133)

1. (a) Positive chemotropism (d) Positive phototropism
   (b) Negative gravitropism (e) Positive thigmotropism
   (c) Positive hydrotropism (f) Positive gravitropism

2. A **tropism** is a growth movement in response to an environmental stimulus, where the direction of the growth response is determined by stimulus direction. Unlike a tropism, the direction of a **nastic response** is independent of the stimulus direction. Nasties are usually quite rapid, often reversible movements. Tropisms are usually slower growth responses.

3. (a) Enables roots to turn and grow down into the soil (where they obtain moisture and nutrients).
   (b) Enables coleoptiles to turn up and grow towards the sunlight (necessary for food manufacture).
   (c) Enables the plant to clamber upwards and grow toward the light instead of possibly becoming smothered by more upright plants.
   (d) Enables pollen tube to locate the micropyle of the embryo sac, and sperm nuclei to fertilise the egg.

Transport and Effect of Auxins (page 134)

1. (a) The growing leaves of the apical bud synthesise auxin in concentrations high enough to suppress the growth of the buds below. Consequently, the main shoot grows more vigorously than the lateral shoots.
   (b) Auxin is a strong promoter of stem elongation and promotes the differentiation of stem tissue.
   (c) Auxin is transported from the tips of the stems and roots to the vascular cambium at other regions of the plant where it promotes cell enlargement and differentiation.
2. Pruning removes the primary source of auxin synthesis and so also the suppressing effect of the apical shoot. Consequently, the lateral shoot growth increases.
3. There are gradients in auxin concentration as a result of growth and transport from source to site of action and this contributes to differential responses in different tissues. In addition, auxin's effect can be different in the presence of other plant hormones. For example the effect of auxin on stem length is stronger if gibberellins are present.

Investigating Phototropism (page 135)

1. (a) Hormone: auxin.
   (b) Response: positive phototropism.
   (c) **Point A**: Cells stay short. **Point B**: Cells elongate.
   (d) Side B
   (e)

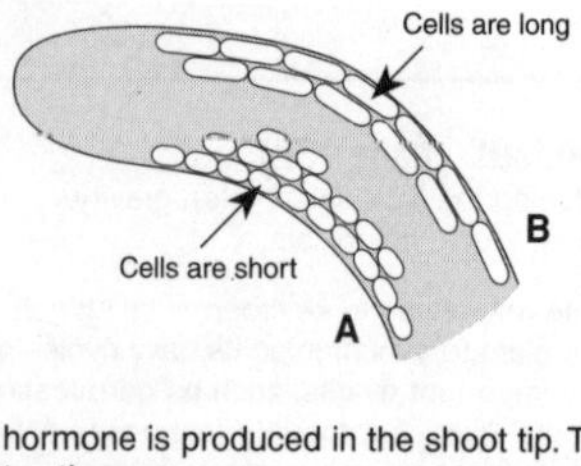

2. The hormone is produced in the shoot tip. The light initiates the response.
3. **Plant A**: The plant will exhibit phototropism and bend towards the sun.
   Plant B: The plant will exhibit no phototropic behaviour and will not bend.

Investigating Gravitropism (page 136)

1. (a) In shoots, more auxin accumulates on the lower side of the shoot. In response to higher auxin levels here, the cells on the lower side of the stem elongate and the shoot tip turns up.
   (b) In roots, the accumulation of auxin on the lower side inhibits elongation (since this is the response of roots to high auxin). The cells on the upper side therefore elongate more than those on the lower side and the root tip turns down.
2. (a) Approximately 10^{-3} mg l^{-1}
   (b) Stem growth is promoted.
3. (a) Stems: A negative geotropic response ensures shoots turn up towards the light (important when light may be absent as when buried deeply in soil).
   (b) Roots: Positive geotropism ensures roots turn down into the soil so that they can begin obtaining the water and minerals required for continued growth.

Hormonal Regulatory Systems (page 137)

1. (a) **Antagonistic hormones**: Two hormones that have contrasting (counteracting) effects on metabolism. Examples: insulin and glucagon, parathormone (increases blood calcium) and calcitonin (lowers blood calcium).
   (b) In general principle, the product of a series of (hormone controlled) reactions controls its own production by turning off the pathway when it reaches a certain level. If there is too little of the product, its production is switched on again.
2. Only the target cells have the appropriate receptors on the membrane to respond to the hormone. Other (nontarget) cells will not be affected.
3. (a) Hormones must circulate in the blood to reach the target cells and a metabolic response must be initiated. This takes some time.
   (b) Hormones bring about a metabolic change and often start a sequence of cascading, interrelated events. Once started, these events take time to conclude. Nervous responses continue only for the time that the stimulation continues.

Cell Signalling (page 138)

1. (a) **Endocrine signalling**, where a hormone is carried in the blood between the endocrine gland/organ where it is produced to target cells.
   (b) **Paracrine signalling**, where cell signalling molecules are released to act on target cells in the immediate vicinity, e.g. at synapses or between cells during development.
   (c) **Autocrine signalling**, where cells produce and react to their own signals (e.g. growth factors from T cells stimulate the production of more T cells).
2. The three signalling types all have in common some kind of chemical messenger or signal molecule (ligand) and a receptor molecule (on the target cells, which may or may not be on the cell producing the signal).

Nervous Regulatory Systems (page 139)

1. (a) The **sensory receptors** receive sensory information (information about the environment) and respond by generating an electrical response (message).
   (b) The **central nervous system** (CNS) processes the sensory input and coordinates an appropriate response (through motor output).
   (c) A system of **effectors** bring about an appropriate response.
   Note: Together these systems function to bring about appropriate (adaptive) responses to the environment

so that homeostasis (steady state) is maintained.

2. (a) and (b) any two in any order:
   - Nervous control involves transmission across synapses, hormonal control involves transport of chemicals in the blood.
   - Nervous control is rapid, hormonal control is slower.
   - Nervous control acts in the short term and its effects are short lived, hormonal control is longer acting.
   - Nervous control is direct and through specific pathways, hormonal control is widespread, affecting target cells throughout the body (although these may be quite specific).
   - Nervous control causes muscular action directly, hormonal control generally acts by changing metabolic activity.

Reflexes (page 140)

1. Higher reasoning is not a preferable feature of reflexes because it would slow down the response time. The adaptive value of reflexes is in allowing a very rapid response to a stimulus.
2. A spinal reflex involves integration within the spinal cord, e.g. knee jerk (monosynaptic) or pain withdrawal (polysynaptic). A cranial reflex involves integration within the brain stem (e.g. pupil reflex).
3. (a) A monosynaptic reflex arc involves just two neurones and one synapse (e.g. knee jerk reflex) and a polysynaptic reflex arc involves two synapses through a relay or interneurone, e.g. pain withdrawal.
   (b) A monosynaptic reflex arc, because there is one less synapse over which diffusion of neurotransmitter must occur.
4. (a) Newborn reflexes equip them with the appropriate survival behaviour in their otherwise helpless state: the rooting reflex helps them to locate a nipple, the suckling reflex insures feeding, the startle reflex induces crying, invoking a parental care response, the grasp reflex ensures they keep contact with (usually) the mother.
   (b) The presence of these reflexes indicates appropriate development. An absence of reflex behaviours in newborns may indicate neural damage or developmental impairment.

The Autonomic Nervous System (page 141)

1. (a) **Sympathetic** NS: Fibres originate from the spinal cord in thoracic and lumbar regions. Preganglionic fibres are short and release acetylcholine. Postganglionic fibres are long and usually liberate noradrenaline.
   (b) **Parasympathetic** NS: Fibres originate from the brainstem and the sacral region of the spinal cord. Preganglionic fibres are long and postganglionic fibres are very short. All parasympathetic fibres (pre- and postganglionic) are cholinergic and liberate acetylcholine.
2. (a) The sympathetic division of the ANS is more active when the body is preparing for action ('fight or flight') while the parasympathetic division is more active in conserving energy and replenishing energy reserves ('feed or breed' or 'rest and digest'). In general, the sympathetic NS stimulates where the parasympathetic inhibits and vice versa.
   (b) Most sympathetic postganglionic nerves release noradrenaline which enters the bloodstream and is deactivated slowly. In contrast, parasympathetic nerves release acetylcholine which is rapidly deactivated at the synapse with short-lived localised effects.
3. Autonomic nervous system controls visceral motor functions through reflex activity. Any of the following:

   Pupil reflex:
   Cranial reflex to light. Stimulation of the eye by bright light causes reflex constriction of the pupil mediated through the parasympathetic nervous system.

   Control of heart rate:
   Increase in arterial pressure causes reflex stimulation of the cardioinhibitory centre through the parasympathetic division, slowing heart rate and decreasing arterial BP to normal. If BP falls, reflex acceleration of the heart takes place: the baroreceptors do not stimulate the cardioinhibitory centre, and the accelerator centre (sympathetic) is free to dominate. A similar reflex (the Bainbridge or right heart reflex) operates in response to increased venous return. Increased return of blood to the heart causes reflex stimulation of the accelerator centre, causing heart rate to increase (sympathetic).

   Control of digestive secretions and gut motility:
   Parasympathetic stimulation increases peristalsis (gut motility), promotes insulin and enzyme secretion and sugar storage. This readies the body for rest. Sympathetic stimulation prepares the body for action by decreasing peristalsis, inhibiting insulin and enzyme secretion and releasing sugar into the bloodstream.
   Note: The enteric nervous system (ENS) is an independent part of the ANS, comprising of special neurones. These neurones are located in specialised bundles in the gut wall and they provide localised reflexes during the digestion of food.
4. Bladder emptying is under reflex control and is stimulated by stretching of the bladder wall. Stretching causes both a conscious desire to urinate and an unconscious reflex contraction of the bladder wall and relaxation of the internal urethral sphincter. The conscious part of the brain also sends impulses to relax the external urethral sphincter. Because both conscious and unconscious controls are involved, urination can be voluntarily stopped and started at will (this control relies on **recognition** of and response to the cues for bladder emptying. This occurs around two years of age).
5. A sudden decrease in blood pressure would result in the sympathetic NS increasing the constriction of the coronary blood vessels and subsequent increase in the rate and force of contraction of the heart. As a result, blood pressure would rise.
6. Inhalation of the drug results in dilation of the bronchioles (airways) in the lungs and the patient is able to breathe more easily.

Control of Heart Rate (page 143)

1. The heart beat originates in the heart muscle itself (it is myogenic) and its rhythm is regulated by the sinoatrial

node (the heart's pacemaker) which spontaneously generates action potentials that spread to the ventricles via the Purkinje fibres.

2. Noradrenaline is released from the axon terminals of the cardiac nerve (sympathetic stimulation) and acts as a neurotransmitter to increase heart rate. Noradrenaline is also released from sympathetic nerves supplying the adrenal medulla, stimulating the release of noadrenaline (and adrenaline) which act as hormones (carried in the blood) to increase cardiac output.

3. Elevated heart rate increases cardiac output, supplying more blood to muscles in preparation for responding to the stress (e.g. running or fighting).

4. (a) Increases heart rate via release of noradrenaline
   (b) Decreases heart rate via release of acetylcholine

5. (a) Increased arterial flow (in aorta and carotid arteries).
   (b) Stretch receptors in carotid sinus and aorta detect an increase in arterial flow and send afferent impulses to the inhibitory centre in the medulla. The inhibitory centre mediates a decrease in heart rate via the vagus nerve (the carotid and aortic reflexes). There is a subsequent decrease in cardiac output and arterial blood pressure.

6. (a) and (b) any of the following in any order:
   - Aortic pressure receptors (baroreceptors) in the wall of the aortic arch respond to increased arterial blood flow in the aorta.
   - Carotid baroreceptors in the carotid sinus respond to increased arterial flow in the carotid artery.
   - Baroreceptors in the vena cava and the right atrium respond to increased venous return (mediates an increase in heart rate - the Bainbridge reflex).

7. (a) Individuals have different tolerances to the same level of a substance (also depends on their previous intakes of other substances such as coffee). Different body mass will affect the response also.
   (b) Controls should drink an energy drink that does not contain guarana.

The Basis of Sensory Perception (page 145)

1. Sensory receptors convert stimulus energy (e.g. electromagnetic radiation) into electrochemical energy (a change in membrane potential).

2. Linking the size of a sensory response to stimulus energy allows the incorporation (into the message) of valuable information about the strength of the stimulus (i.e. is the stimulus worth responding to or not).

3. Sensory adaptation allows the nervous system to cease responding to constant stimuli that do not change in intensity. This prevents nervous system overstimulation and allows constant, background sensory information to be ignored.

4. (a) Generator potentials are localised depolarisations and are graded (of different sub-threshold magnitude). Unlike action potentials they are not self-propagating.
   (b) It is important that a receptor does not respond to stimuli at sub-threshold intensities as this could mean the receptor would be responding inappropriately and too often. **Note**: The threshold level is a stimulus intensity that is established through natural selection as appropriate in the prevailing environment and (like other biological responses) is subject to change over time.

The Structure of the Eye (page 146)

1. (a) **Cornea**: Responsible for most of the refraction (bending) of the incoming light.
   (b) **Ciliary body**: Secretes the aqueous humour.
   (c) **Retina**: The photosensitive region of the eye containing the photoreceptor cells (rods and cones) which respond to the incoming light.
   (d) **Iris**: Regulates the amount of light entering the eye for vision in bright and dim light.
   (e) **Vitreous and aqueous humours**: Help to maintain the shape of the eye and assist in refraction.

2. (a) **Accommodation** (changes to the shape of the lens) so that a sharp image is formed on the retina.
   (b) Accommodation is achieved by the action of the ciliary muscles pulling on the elastic lens and changing its shape. **Note**: When the ciliary muscle contracts there is decreased pressure on the suspensory ligament and the lens becomes more convex (to focus on near objects). When the ciliary muscle relaxes there is increased tension on the suspensory ligament and the lens is pulled into a thinner shape (to focus on distant objects).

3. The **blind spot** is where all the nerve fibres leave the eye as the optic nerve so there are no photoreceptor cells there (hence "blind"). In contrast, the **fovea** has the greatest density of photoreceptor cells and hence it is the point of most acute vision.

The Physiology of Vision (page 147)

1. (a) The retina is the layer of light sensitive tissue lining the inner surface of the eye. It comprises several layers of neurones, including the photoreceptor rods and cones, interconnected by synapses. Light induces the production of neural signals in the rods and cones, which are processed by other neurones of the retina.
   (b) The optic nerve is formed from the axons of the retinal ganglion cells, which carry the processed neural signals, the form of action potentials, from the retina through the optic chiasma to the visual cortex in the cerebrum. It also contains the blood vessels supplying the retina.

2. Visual acuity is greatest in the central fovea as this is the area of greatest density of cones; the photoreceptor cells specialised for high visual acuity, as well as colour vision. Rods are absent in the central fovea.

3.

Feature	Rod cells	Cone cells
Visual pigment(s):	Rhodopsin (no colour vision)	Iodopsin (three types)
Visual acuity:	Low	High
Overall function:	Vision in dim light, high sensitivity	Colour vision, vision in bright light

4. (a)-(c) in any order
   (a) **Photoreceptor cells (rods and cones)** respond to light by producing generator potentials.
   (b) **Bipolar neurones** form synapses with the rods and cones and transmit the changes in membrane

potential to the ganglion cells. Each cone synapses with one bipolar (=high acuity) whereas each rod synapses with many bipolar cells (=high sensitivity).

(c) **Ganglion cells** synapse with the bipolar cells and respond with depolarisation and generation of action potentials. Their axons form the optic nerve.

5. (a) **Horizontal cells** are interconnecting neurones that help to integrate and regulate the input from multiple photoreceptor cells. They enhance information about contrast.
   (b) **Amacrine cells** form synapses with bipolar cells and work laterally to affect output from the bipolar cells, enhancing information about light level.

6. Each **rod** cell synapses with a number of bipolar cells and this gives poor acuity but high sensitivity. Each **cone** cell synapses with only one bipolar cell and this gives high acuity but poor sensitivity.

7. (a) A photochemical pigment molecule contained in the membranes of the photoreceptor cells that undergoes a structural change when exposed to light (and is therefore light-sensitive).
   (b) Rhodopsin in rods and iodopsin in cones.

8. Light falling on the retina causes structural changes in the photopigments in the rods and cones. These changes lead to the development of graded electrical signals (hyperpolarisations) which spread from the rods and cones, via the bipolar neurones, to the ganglion cells. The ganglion cells respond by depolarisation and transmit action potentials to the brain.

Neurone Structure and Function (page 149)

1. See the completed table below
2. (a) Myelination increases the speed of impulse conduction.
   (b) Oligodendrocytes
   (c) Schwann cells
   (d) Neurones in the PNS frequently have to transmit over long distances so speed of impulse conduction is critical to efficient function.
3. Myelin prevents ions from entering or leaving the axon along myelinated segments and so prevents leakage of charge across the neurone membrane. The current is carried in the cytoplasm so that the action potential at one node (gap in the sheath) is sufficient to trigger an action potential at the next. Myelin has another advantage too in reducing energy expenditure since fewer ions overall need to be pumped to restore resting potential after an action potential has passed.
4. (a) Faster conduction speeds enable more rapid responses to stimuli.
   (b) Increasing axon diameter increases conduction velocity because it reduces the longitudinal resistance, so local currents can spread further.
5. The destruction of the myelin prevents those (previously myelinated) axons from conducting. Without insulation, the neurone membrane leaks ions and the local current is attenuated and insufficient to depolarise the next node. Note: myelinated axons only have gated channels at their nodes, so action potentials can only be generated at node regions in those axons that were previously myelinated.

Action Potentials (page 151)

1. An action potential is a self-regenerating depolarisation (electrochemical signal) that allows excitable cells (such as muscle and nerve cells) to carry a signal over a (varying) distance.
2. (a) The ability to conduct electrical impulses.
   (b) They cannot conduct electrical impulses.
3. An **action potential** passes along a nerve because the depolarisation occurring in one region of the axon makes the next region of the axon more permeable to sodium ions (and more likely to conduct the impulse).
4. Because the refractory period makes the neurone unable to respond for a brief period after an action potential has passed, the impulse can pass in only one direction along the nerve (away from the cell body).
5. The nervous system interprets nerve impulses correctly because it records where they have come from and "knows" where they go to. Different regions of the brain are responsible for sorting out, interpreting, and integrating the nerve impulses from different sources.
6. NOTE: Attentive students will notice that this trace does not perfectly match the idealised schematic of an action potential (namely the hyperpolarisation does not fall below threshold and resting potential is more positive than the starting resting potential). Differences in electrophysiological techniques used in recording lead to departures from the schematic. In this case, the real action potential is sitting atop a voltage offset caused by the current pulse used to stimulate the axon.
   (a) B: Membrane depolarisation
   D: Hyperpolarisation
   E: Return to resting potential
   C: Repolarisation
   A: The membrane's resting potential
   (b) Point 1: Stimulus causes opening of Na^+ channels and Na^+ begins to flow into the cell.

	Sensory neurone	Interneurone	Motor neurone
Length of fibres	Long dendrites, short axon	Short dendrites, long or short axon	Short dendrites, long axons
Location	Dendrites outside the spinal cord, cell body in spinal ganglion	Entirely within the CNS	Dendrites and cell body in the spinal cord; axon outside the spinal cord.
Function	Conduct impulse to CNS	Connect sensory & motor neurones	Conduct impulse to effector (muscle or gland)

(c) Rapid Na^+ influx = rapid depolarisation.

Cholinergic Synapses (page 153)

1. A **synapse** is a junction between the end of one axon and the dendrite or cell body of a receiving neurone. **Note**: A synapse can also occur between the end of one axon and a muscle cell (neuromuscular junction).
2. Arrival of a nerve impulse at the end of the axon causes an influx of calcium. This induces the vesicles to release their neurotransmitter into the cleft.
3. Delay at the synapse is caused by the time it takes for the neurotransmitter to diffuse across the gap (synaptic cleft) between neurones.
4. (a) Neurotransmitter (NT) is degraded into component molecules by enzyme activity on the membrane of the receiving neurone (in this case, acetylcholinesterase acts on Ach to produce acetyl and choline). This reference is to the cholinergic synapse pictured. Continued action of the NT at adrenergic synapses is prevented by reuptake of the NT (noradrenaline) by the presynaptic neurone.
   (b) The neurotransmitter must be deactivated so that it does not continue to stimulate the receiving neurone (continued stimulation would lead to depletion of neurotransmitter and fatigue of the nerve). Deactivation allows recovery of the neurone so that it can respond to further impulses.
5. Function of acetylcholine (either of):
   - It occurs at the synapse between motor neurones and muscle cells, where it causes depolarisation of the muscle cell (and leads to muscle contraction).
   - Ach is released by all parasympathetic fibres (autonomic nervous system) where it may cause an excitatory or inhibitory response (depending on the postsynaptic receptor with which it interacts). NOTE: Ach is also released by preganglionic fibres in the sympathetic division of the ANS.
6. The amount of neurotransmitter released influences the response of the receiving cell (response strength is proportional to amount of neurotransmitter released).

Integration at Synapses (page 154)

1. Integration refers to the interpretation and coordination (by the central nervous system) of inputs from many sources (inputs may be inhibitory or excitatory).
2. (a) **Summation**: The additive effect of presynaptic inputs (impulses) in the postsynaptic cell (neurone or muscle fibre).
   (b) **Spatial summation** refers to the summation of impulses from **separate** axon terminals arriving simultaneously at the postsynaptic cell. **Temporal summation** refers to the arrival of several impulses from a **single** axon terminal in rapid succession (the postsynaptic potentials are so close together in time that they can sum to generate an action potential).
3. (a) **Acetylcholine** is the NT involved; arrival of an action potential at the neuromuscular junction causes the release of Ach from the synaptic knobs.
   (b) Ach causes **depolarisation** of the postsynaptic membrane (in this case,the sarcolemma). **Note**: The depolarisation in response to the arrival of an action potential at the postsynaptic cell is essentially the same as that occurring at any excitatory synapse involving Ach neurotransmitter.

Drugs at Synapses (page 155)

1. (a) and (b) any of in any order:
   - Drug can act as a direct agonist, binding to and activating Ach receptors on the postsynaptic membrane, e.g. nicotine.
   - Drug can act as an indirect agonist, preventing the breakdown of Ach, thereby causing continued response in the postsynaptic cell, e.g. therapeutic drugs used to treat Alzheimer's disease.
   - Drug can act as an antagonist, competing for Ach binding sites and reducing or blocking the response of the postsynaptic cell, e.g. atropine or curare.
2. Any one of:
   - Drug can act as an indirect agonist, preventing the reuptake of noradrenaline by the presynaptic cell, thereby prolonging the response in the postsynaptic cell, e.g. cocaine and amphetamines.
   - Drug can act as a direct antagonist, competing for adrenergic β receptors on the postsynaptic membrane and blocking impulse transmission, e.g. β blockers used to treat hypertension.
3. Atropine and curare are direct antagonists because they compete for the same binding sites (as Ach) on the postsynaptic membrane (hence **direct)** and they block sodium influx so that impulses are not generated (hence **antagonist** = against the usual action).
4. Curare is used to cause flaccid paralysis (relaxed or without tone) to the isolated abdominal region in order to facilitate operative procedure (of course, the drug is administered as a carefully produced formulation).

Muscle Structure and Function (page 157)

1. **Smooth muscle**, also called involuntary muscle, has spindle shaped cells with one central nucleus per cell and a smooth appearance with no striations. Its contractions are diffuse and it is not under conscious control so it is involved in movement of visceral organs such as the gut. **Striated** (skeletal) **muscle** is voluntary and is responsible for the skeletal muscle movement over which we have conscious control. It has a striated or striped appearance and the cells are multinucleate with peripheral nuclei. **Cardiac muscle** is involuntary muscle responsible for the contraction of the heart s. Although it is striated, it does not fatigue in the same way as skeletal muscle. There is one nucleus per cell and structures called intercalated discs (electrical junctions) join individual cells.
2. (a) The banding pattern results from the overlap pattern of the thick and thin filaments (dark = thick and thin filaments overlapping, light = no overlap).
   (b) **I band**: Becomes narrower as more filaments overlap and the area of non-overlap decreases.
   H zone: Disappears as the overlap becomes maximal (no region of only thick filaments).
   Sarcomere: Shortens progressively as the overlap becomes maximal.
3. Protects the muscle from friction and provides

structural integrity to the muscle tissue. The perimysium (surrounding the fascicles) may also be involved in transmitting contractile movements across the muscle.

4. The all-or-none response refers to the way in which an individual muscle fibre contracts maximally (if the stimulus is strong enough) or not at all (if it is not).

5. Without dystrophin there is no structural link between the muscle fibres and the extracellular matrix. Calcium penetrates the plasma membrane (sarcolemma) of the muscle cells and damages them, eventually destroying the muscle cells (fibres).

The Sliding Filament Theory (page 159)

1. (a) **Myosin**: Has a moveable head that provides a power stroke when activated.
   (b) **Actin**: Two protein molecules twisted in a double helix shape that form the thin filament of a myofibril.
   (c) **Calcium ions**: Bind to the blocking molecules, causing them to move and expose the myosin binding site.
   (d) **Troponin-tropomyosin**: Bind to actin molecule in a way that prevents myosin head from forming a cross bridge.
   (e) **ATP**: Supplies energy for flexing of the myosin head (power stroke).

2. (a) By changing the frequency of stimulation, so that fibres receive impulses at a greater rate (frequency summation).
   (b) By changing the number and size of motor units recruited (a few motor units = a small contraction, maximum number of motor units = maximum contraction).

3. (a) Calcium ions and ATP.
   (b) Calcium ions are released from a store in the sarcoplasmic reticulum when an action potential arrives. ATP is present in the muscle fibre and is hydrolysed by ATPase enzymes on the myosin.

The Mechanics of Movement (page 160)

1. Muscles can only contract and relax, therefore they can only pull on a bone; they cannot push it. To produce movement, two muscles must act as **antagonistic** pairs to move a bone to and from different positions. To raise a limb, the flexor contracts pulling the limb bone up (extensor relaxed). To lower the limb, the extensor contracts, pulling the limb down (flexor relaxed).

2. (a) Radius
   (b) Ulna
   (b) Rotation of ulna and radius

Energy for Muscle Contraction (page 161)

1. Lactic acid quickly builds up as a waste product of the glycolytic pathway. Lactic acid inhibits glycogen breakdown and impedes muscular contraction, so the time period for its use is limited.

2. **Energy systems**:
   ATP-CP
   ATP supplied by: Breakdown of CP
   Duration of ATP supply: Short (3-15 s)
   Glycolytic
   ATP supplied by: Anaerobic breakdown of glycogen
   Duration of ATP supply: A few minutes at most.
   Oxidative
   ATP supplied by: Complete aerobic (oxidative) breakdown of glycogen to CO_2 and water.
   Duration of ATP supply: Prolonged but dependent on ability to supply oxygen to the muscles (fitness).

3. (a) Shaded region **A**: Oxygen deficit: the amount of oxygen needed for aerobic supply but not supplied by breathing i.e. an oxygen deficit builds up.
   (b) Shaded region **B**: Oxygen debt: the extra oxygen required (taken in) despite the drop in energy demand. The debt is used to replace oxygen reserves, restore CP, and break down lactic acid.
   Note: Both components (deficit and debt) are often used synonymously (as oxygen debt) although they are not quite the same. The deficit is the oxygen shortfall incurred during exercise; the debt is the amount of oxygen required to restore oxygen and energy stores to resting levels. Their values are not necessarily the same.

4. Oxygen uptake does not immediately return to resting levels because of the extra oxygen required to restore oxygen and energy levels (the oxygen debt).

5. Oxygen supply is increased by increased rate and depth of breathing (increasing gas exchange rate) and increased blood flow (increased gas transport).

6. Lactic acid levels in the blood rise for a time after exercise because the lactic acid is transported in the blood from the muscles (where it has accumulated) to the liver, where it is metabolised to CO_2 and water.

Muscle Tone and Posture (page 163)

1. (a) Muscle tone is the continuous and passive partial contraction of muscles giving a firm appearance.
   (b) At any one time, a few fibres in a muscle are always contracting involuntarily (different fibres at different times).

2. (a) The **muscle spindle organ** monitors the degree of stretch (contraction) in a muscle and provides information to bring about adjustment of contraction.
   (b) **Intrafusal fibres parallel to extrafusal fibres**: When the muscle relaxes, it lengthens and the muscle spindle is stretched. The stretching results in a reflex adjustment of contraction (usually to maintain tone).
   Sensory neurones in non-contractile region: When non-contractile portion is stretched (it cannot, itself, adjust its length), sensory neurones are stimulated.
   Motor neurone synapses: When the motor impulses arrive to adjust state of contraction, both the extrafusal and intrafusal fibres are adjusted appropriately.

Muscle Fatigue (page 164)

1. Lactic acid accumulation in muscle tissue results in lowered pH and inhibition of cellular activity.

2. (a) Fall in ATP production
   (b) Fall in calcium release

3. In a long distance race, such as a marathon, ATP continues to be produced **aerobically** until all energy supplies are exhausted. In a sprint ATP is produced **anaerobically** until the oxygen debt has been repaid.

Muscle Physiology and Performance (page 165)

1. (a)-(c) Any three, in any order. Endurance training improves the oxidative function of muscle through:
   - Improved oxidation of glycogen, which increases the capacity of the muscle to generate ATP aerobically.
   - Increased capacity of the muscle to oxidise fats, which allows glycogen to be used at a slower rate.
   - Increased myoglobin content in the muscle, which stores oxygen and aids oxygen delivery to mitochondria.
   - An increase in the number of capillaries surrounding muscle fibres increases oxygen delivery and removal of wastes.
   - An increase in the size and density of mitochondria in the muscle.
   - An increase in the concentration and activity of Krebs cycle enzymes improves capacity for aerobic respiration.
   - An increase in fibre size which can accommodate an increase in mitochondria, myoglobin, and glycogen storage.

2. **Fast twitch** fibres are large, pale fibres with rapid contraction rates, rapid rates of ATP production, and high power generation. They work anaerobically, but fatigue quickly, and these properties suit them to short bursts of activity where maximal force is required quickly (as in sprinting or power lifting). **Slow twitch** fibres, in contrast, are darker (red) due to the presence of large amounts of myoglobin, they are small in diameter and have a slower rate of ATP production and a slower contraction rate. They work aerobically, but fatigue slowly, so they are suited to activities where endurance and prolonged activity at a sustainable level is required. **Note**: Fast twitch fibres will be (preferentially) developed and recruited in sprint trained athletes. Slow twitch fibres will be (preferentially) developed and recruited in endurance trained athletes. Muscle contains a mix of fibre types, providing the capacity for both explosive effort and endurance.

Principles of Homeostasis (page 167)

1. **Receptors** (detect stimuli), **control and coordination centre** (integration of signals and coordination of response), **effectors** (implement appropriate response).

2. Negative feedback mechanisms enable maintenance of a steady state internal environment despite fluctuations in the external environment (e.g. rising air temperature). Negative feedback mechanisms are self-correcting so that physiological systems are stabilised against excessive change.

3. (a) Positive feedback has a role in accelerating a physiological process to bring about a particular required response. Examples include (1) elevation in body temperature (fever) to accelerate protective immune responses, (2) positive feedback between oestrogen and LH to leading to an LH surge and ovulation, (3) positive feedback between oxytocin and uterine contractions: oxytocin causes uterine contraction and stretching of the cervix, which causes more release of oxytocin and so on until the delivery of the infant.
   (b) Positive feedback is inherently unstable because it causes an escalation in the physiological response, pushing it outside the tolerable physiological range. Compare this with negative feedback, which is self correcting and causes the system to return to the steady state.
   (c) Positive feedback loops are normally ended by a resolution of situation causing the initial stimulation. For example, the positive feedback loop between oestrogen and LH leading to ovulation is initiated by high oestrogen levels and ended when these fall quickly after ovulation, prompting a resumption of negative feedback mechanisms. In childbirth, once the infant is delivered, the stretching of the cervix ceases and so too does the stimulation for more oxytocin release.
   (d) When positive feedback continues unchecked, it can lead to physiological collapse. One example includes unresolved fever. If an infection is not brought under control (e.g. by the body's immune system mechanisms or medical intervention), body temperature will continue to rise and can lead to seizures, neurological damage, and death.

4. Sometimes the metabolic responses required to maintain a steady state are too disparate to be brought about by one hormone; it is more physiologically efficient to control responses in different directions with **counter-regulatory hormones**. This is especially true when the homeostatic process is naturally subject to sudden wide variations, which require different responses to stabilise. For example, insulin is released in response to elevated blood sugar and induces cellular uptake of glucose and synthesis of glycogen. Glucagon is released in response to low blood glucose and induces release of glucose from stores.

Maintaining Homeostasis (page 169)

1. Two mechanisms operating to restore homeostasis after infection ((a) and (b) any two of):
   - Immune system response with the production of antibodies against the antigens of the pathogen (humoral response).
   - Immune system response with the production of T cells which recognise the antigens of the pathogen and destroy them directly (cell-mediated response).
   - Local inflammatory response (redness, pain, swelling, heat) at the site of infection.
   - Fever (widespread increase in body temperature).
   - The production of antimicrobial substances like interferon and interleukin-1.
   - Phagocytosis of pathogen by white blood cells.

   All the above aim to destroy the pathogen and/or its toxins and assist a return to homeostasis.

For Q. 2.-4., more explanatory detail than required is given.

2. Mechanisms by which responses to stimuli are brought about and coordinated:
   (a) **Hormonal response** to stimuli: Endocrine glands respond to a stimulus (e.g. a nerve impulse or another hormone or metabolite) by producing hormones which bring about an appropriate physiological response. **For example**, nervous stimulation of the adrenal glands when the body

receives a stressful stimulus causes the release of adrenaline. This hormone causes mobilisation of glucose in muscle and liver cells, increases heart rate and directs blood away from nonessential organs. These responses help the body react to the stress situation.

(b) **Nervous response** to stimuli: Direct stimulation of nerves from a sensory receptor causes a reaction to the stimulus. This may be a response requiring interpretation of the message by the brain or it may be a reflex (an automatic response to a stimulus involving only 2 or 3 neurones), e.g. pain withdrawal.

3. Maintaining water and ion balance by:
   (a) Water and ions are taken in with food and drink, helping to replace that lost through urine, faeces, and sweat. The digestive organs and all of the digestive hormones (e.g. amylase in the mouth, pepsin in the stomach, trypsin in the small intestine) are all involved in breaking down food and facilitating absorption into the bloodstream.
   (b) The kidney is the primary regulator of fluid and ions. When large quantities of fluid must be excreted, the kidney produces large amounts of dilute urine. When water must be conserved, small amounts of concentrated urine are produced. ADH (antidiuretic hormone) causes more water to be reabsorbed from the kidney (causing a more concentrated urine). ADH increases when blood water levels are low. Essential ions (and glucose) are retained by active reabsorption from the kidney tubules. Another hormone, aldosterone from the adrenal glands, increases the absorption of sodium ions.
   Note: Water and ions are lost via sweat and water is lost in breathing. These losses are compensated for by the homeostatic role of the kidney. Note that sweating is a mechanism for thermoregulation. It is not usually an important way to rid the body of excessive water and salts.

4. Regulating respiratory gases during exercise by:
   (a) **Increasing breathing rate**. This increases both the rate of oxygen entering the lungs and the rate at which carbon dioxide leaves. It also increases the rate of loading and unloading of oxygen and carbon dioxide into and out of the bloodstream.
   (b) **Increasing the heart rate**. This increases blood flow which facilitates the loading and unloading of oxygen and carbon dioxide into and out of the bloodstream. It also increases the speed of delivery of oxygen to working tissues (e.g. muscles) and speeds up the removal of carbon dioxide and other waste products of metabolism.

Control of Body Temperature (page 171)

1. (a) A **homeothermic endotherm** maintains a constant (usually high) body temperature despite environmental fluctuations. It does this using internal sources of energy (metabolic activity).
   (b) Many terrestrial lizards and snakes regulate their body temperature to within quite narrow limits using behavioural mechanisms. Their body temperature does not simply fluctuate with ambient temperature.

2. (a) Letting body temperature fluctuate with the environment saves a great deal of energy because the animal does not have to maintain body temperature against environmental variation.
   (b) Ectothermy represents an energy saving since ectotherms are not physiologically committed to maintaining a high metabolic rate. Lower metabolic rates are advantageous when food supplies are low (less energy is required to sustain the animal).

3. Endotherms that undergo torpor usually do so when food supplies are scarce and/or when the metabolic cost of maintaining activity is likely to be prohibitively high (e.g. during very cold weather). Lowering metabolic rates at these times saves energy and allows them to survive until conditions are more favourable.

4. (a) Ectotherm's body temperature increases steadily with increasing ambient temperature. Endotherms maintain a high, constant body temperature despite changes in the environmental temperature.
   (b) An poikilothermic ectotherm would be restricted to temperatures below about 40-45°C because above this point its body temperature would continue to rise to a state of physiological heat stress.
   (c) Optimum temperature range for an endotherm is from 18° or 19°C to 36°C. Between these temperatures, oxygen consumption, and therefore energy expenditure, is lowest.
   (d) At temperatures below 15°C the energetic costs of thermoregulation for an endotherm increase markedly because the environmental temperature is low compared with the preferred constant body temperature and more energy is required to maintain body temperature against heat loss. At temperatures above 35°C the energetic costs of thermoregulation also increase because large amounts of energy begin to be used to dissipate excess heat and prevent further heat gain.
   (e) For ectotherms, the energetic costs of temperature regulation increase steadily with the environmental temperature because as the environmental temperature increases so too does the metabolic rate of the animal. Increased metabolic rate equates to increased energetic expenditure and higher oxygen consumption.

Mechanisms of Thermoregulation (page 173)

1. (a) Water transmits heat away from the body very rapidly, therefore it has a great cooling capacity.
   (b) Any two of: Countercurrent heat exchange systems in fins and flippers, insulated body surfaces of thick fat, large body size.
   (c) Large body size reduces the surface area (compared to volume) over which heat can be lost.
   (d) Any of: High heat production through high metabolic rate, consumption of large amounts of food, hibernation or torpor during winter periods.

2. (a) Thick hair reduces heat loss by trapping an insulating layer of air between the animal and the cooler environment. The insulating layer of hair also reduces heat gain from the environment.
   (b) Different fur thicknesses allow an animal to expose or cover thinner areas to allow for greater of lower heat loss depending on needs.
   (c) Related species at low altitude could be expected to have less thick and less dense fur covering than animals at high altitude.
   (d) They have a thick layer of fat (blubber) underneath the skin. In addition, they are usually large.

3. (a) Use of countercurrent heat exchanges in fast swimming fish allows them to maintain a higher operating temperature in their main swimming muscles. This enables faster metabolic activity and fast, sustained swimming.
(b) These animals ingest large volumes of flesh in their diet, without chewing. A higher temperature around the gut allows them to increase the rate of digestion so that assimilation rates do not lag too much behind the rate at which food is ingested.

4. (a) Animals may group together to retain body heat. By creating a large single mass, heat loss is reduced.
(b) Penguins, honeybees, livestock (sheep, cattle).

Thermoregulation in Humans (page 175)

1. Body temperature reduced by (a and b any two of): • Sweating (cooling by evaporation) • Reducing activity • Behavioural mechanisms such as removing clothing or seeking shade • Increasing blood flow to skin (leads to increased radiation from the skin surface) .

2. (a) **Hypothalamus**: Monitors temperature changes in the body and coordinates appropriate responses to counteract the changes.
(b) **Skin**: Detects changes in skin temperature and relays the information to the hypothalamus. In response to input from the hypothalamus, muscles and capillaries in the skin act as effectors to bring about an appropriate thermoregulatory response.
(c) **Nervous input to effectors**: (from hypothalamus) brings about (through stimulation of muscles) an appropriate thermoregulatory response (e.g. raising hairs, constricting blood vessels).
(d) **Hormones**: Mediate a change in metabolic rate through their general action on body cells (adrenaline and thyroxine increase metabolic rate).

Second Messenger Systems (page 176)

1. The signalling cascade that is initiated depends on the receptor type that binds the signal molecule (and first messenger) adrenaline. If the target cell type (e.g. smooth muscle) possesses α-receptors, adrenaline activates the G protein, which directly brings about the cellular response. If the target cell type (e.g. liver cell) possesses β-receptors, adrenaline links the activation of the G protein to the cellular response (e.g. glycogen breakdown) through a second messenger, cyclic AMP.

2. The binding of a hormone molecule to a receptor, initiates a series of reactions within the cell that result in, often far reaching, effects. In many cases, hormones exert their effects by influencing the enzymes associated with membranes or genetic control.

3. Both involve a specific recognition reaction. In the case of enzymes, recognition and binding to the substrate; in the case of hormones, recognition and binding to a cellular receptor.

Control of Blood Glucose (page 177)

1. (a) Stimulus: Rise in the levels of glucose in the blood above a set level (about 100 mg per 100 cm^3).
(b) Stimulus: Fall in blood glucose levels below a set level (about 75 mg per 100 cm^3).
(c) Glucagon brings about the production (and subsequent release) of glucose from the liver by the breakdown of glycogen and the synthesis of glucose from amino acids.
(d) Insulin increases glucose uptake by cells (thereby lowering blood glucose) and brings about production of glycogen and fat from glucose in the liver.

2. Negative feedback mechanisms prevent excessive fluctuations in blood glucose (BG). Fall in BG triggers glucagon release, BG rises, normal BG is restored, and glucagon release stops. Rise in BG triggers insulin release, BG falls, normal BG is restored, and insulin release stops.

3. Glycogen stores in the liver become depleted and **fats** remain the next most favoured energy source available to the body. **Note**: Metabolism of fats alone for energy over an extended period of time can result in metabolic acidosis and is not recommended.

4. (a) Glycogenesis: the production of glycogen from glucose in the liver, stimulated by insulin.
(b) Glycogenolysis: breakdown of glycogen to produce glucose, stimulated by adrenaline and glucagon.
(c) Gluconeogenesis: the production of glucose from non-carbohydrate sources, stimulated by adrenaline and glucocorticoid hormones.

5. (a) Adrenaline: Stimulates breakdown of glycogen and synthesis of glucose from non-carbohydrate sources such as fats and amino acids.
(b) Glucagon: Stimulates conversion (breakdown) of glycogen to glucose.
(c) Insulin: Promotes glycogen storage by stimulating production of glycogen from glucose.

Diabetes Mellitus (page 179)

1. With a lack of insulin (or lack of response to insulin), the body's cells are unable to take up glucose from the blood and, as a result, blood glucose remains high.

2. Type 1 diabetes arises because of a complete lack of insulin (as a result of destruction of the beta cells during childhood) and is treated primarily with the regular injection of insulin to enable the body to take up and utilise glucose after meals. Type 2 diabetes is the result of insulin resistance, i.e. the cells no longer respond to insulin or respond at too low a level. Treatment is centred around controlling the factors exacerbating the diabetes: controlling weight and diet, and increasing exercise, although anti-diabetic drugs and insulin therapy may be needed in severe cases,

3. The increase in type 2 diabetes has been associated with the increasing trend towards sedentary lifestyles, and the increasing proportion of overweight and obese people in the population. This proportion is now very high (more than 50% in some cases), so much so that young people are increasingly being diagnosed with type 2 diabetes (in previous decades, it was a disease of late middle age).

4. (a) Difficulties encountered include:
– difficulties in promoting differentiation of the stem cells (the correct culturing environment, and the correct growth factors, delivered at the correct time,

are absolutely necessary), especially if the stem cells are not ESCs.
- inadequate levels of insulin production, or (in transformed cells) inadequate expression of the gene once inserted.

(b) Adult stem cells are taken from cord blood or bone marrow whereas ESCs are derived from early stage embryos, which (to date) are destroyed by the process. This causes issues of embryonic rights from those concerned with the sacrifice of a potential life.

The Oestrous Cycle (page 181)

1. Peaks in FSH are associated with declines in oestrogen. This is because FSH promotes follicle development, and the follicle secretes oestrogen, but as each (intermediate) follicle dies, oestrogen drops and allows FSH to increase (negative feedback regulation).
2. Fertilisation of the egg is most likely around 24 hours after ovulation.
3. For the follicle to fully develop, oestrogen levels must be high enough to induce the production of luteinising hormone (responsible for final development and ovulation of the egg). Progesterone inhibits the production of oestrogen, and only when progesterone levels fall can the follicle fully develop. Note: It seems that the follicle that is selected to develop is often the one that naturally produces a lot of oestrogen. This predisposes it towards becoming the dominant follicle.

Control of the Oestrous Cycle (page 182)

1. The hypothalamus is central to regulating the release of reproductive hormones from the anterior pituitary through the secretion of GnRH. GnRH induces the release of FSH and LH from the anterior pituitary, which in turn control follicle growth and development, maintenance of the corpus luteum, and ovulation.
2. (a) FSH stimulates the development of the follicle which produces oestrogen.
   (b) LH induces development of the corpus luteum and ovulation in the follicular phase.
   (c) Progesterone inhibits the release of GnRH (therefore LH) to support the corpus luteum during the first part of the cycle. High progesterone after 16 days induces release of prostaglandin from the uterus and brings the luteal phase to an end.
   (d) Oestrogen inhibits the release of FSH via negative feedback. Positive feedback between oestrogen and LH during the follicular phase induces the LH surge, which results in ovulation.
3. The corpus luteum is short lived but produces progesterone and is responsible for maintaining the pregnancy until the full development of the placenta.
4. (a) Negative feedback loops control the development of the early stages of the oestrus cycle while a positive feedback loop results in the LH surge and ovulation characterising the follicular phase. During the luteal phase of the cycle, negative feedback inhibits LH/FSH release from the anterior pituitary, regulating follicular development. Positive feedback between progesterone and PG from the uterus causes the CL to break down, ending the luteal phase. Positive feedback of oestrogen on the hypothalamus escalates the LH release and leads to the LH surge responsible for ovulation.
   (b)) If the cow becomes pregnant, the developing embryo sends chemical signals to the uterus not to produce prostaglandins. The CL continues to produce progesterone, maintaining the pregnancy and inhibiting oestrogen production and (therefore also) suppressing further ovulation.
5. Prostaglandin causes the destruction of the CL. This lowers progesterone levels and allows levels of oestrogen to rise.
6. (a) Detection of standing oestrus allows a farmer to identify when a cow is ready to be inseminated and helps to maximise calf production.
   (b) Using oestrogen to induce ovulation at the same time allows a farmer to regulate the timing of calving, since all cows will calve around the same time. It also maximises profits by having all calves ready for market at the same time.

The Genetic Code (page 185)

1. (a) DNA: ATG GGT TAC CTG AGG GTA ATA CGG GCA CTT TAG
   (b) mRNA: AUG GGU UAC CUG AGG GUA AUA CGG GCA CUU UAG
   Amino acids: Met Gly Tyr Leu Arg Val Iso Arg Ala Leu STOP
2. (a) Start: AUG STOP: UAA, UAG, UGA
   (b) They indicate the starting and finishing points on the mRNA (as dictated by the DNA) for the instructions enabling the construction of a polypeptide chain.

Transcription (page 186)

1. mRNA carries a copy of the genetic instructions from the DNA in the nucleus to ribosomes in the cytoplasm. The rate of protein synthesis can be increased by making many copies of identical mRNA from the same piece of DNA.
2. (a) AUG (b) UAA, UAG, UGA
3. (a) AUG AUC GGC GCU AAA
   (b) AUG UUC GGA UAU UUU

Gene Expression (page 187)

1. In **prokaryotic** gene expression, RNA is translated into protein almost as fast as it is transcribed; there is no nucleus therefore no separation of the transcription and translation processes. The presence of introns in a prokaryotic genome would interfere with protein function because there would be no time between transcription and translation to splice them out.
   In contrast, **eukaryotic** gene expression involves production of a primary RNA transcript from which the introns are removed. There is sufficient time for this to take place because transcription and translation occur inside and outside the nucleus respectively. **Note**: Evidence in support of this: Prokaryote DNA consists almost entirely of protein-coding genes and their regulatory sequences with very little non-protein coding DNA. Eukaryotic DNA comprises large amounts of non-protein coding sequences, much of which we now know codes for functional (regulatory) RNAs.

2. In the new view of eukaryotic gene expression, the so-called "junk DNA", traditionally regarded as non-functional, is considered to play a necessary role in the eukaryote cell. In fact, there is a good correlation between the amount of non-protein coding DNA a species has and its complexity. Although this DNA does not code for proteins, its does code for RNA molecules with regulatory functions (some of these involving regulation of the genome itself). What's more, in the new view of gene expression, not all of the exonic RNA is translated into protein; some contributes to regulatory microRNAs. In the old view, all exonic RNA was thought to code for proteins.

3. The one gene-one protein model is still appropriate for prokaryotes because, in the absence of introns, RNA transcripts are translated directly into proteins. Because of the small size of prokaryotic genomes and their one site of protein synthesis, there is very little non-protein coding DNA present.

Translation (page 189)

1. AUG AUC GGC GCU AAA
2. (a) 61
   (b) There are 64 possible codons for mRNA, but three are terminator codons. 61 codons for mRNA require 61 tRNAs each with a complementary codon.

Protein Synthesis Summary (page 190)

1. A DNA
   B Free nucleotides
   C RNA polymerase enzyme
   D mRNA
   E Nuclear membrane
   F Nuclear pore
   G tRNA
   H Amino acids
   I Ribosome
   J Polypeptide chain

2. **8** tRNA molecule is recharged with another amino acid of the same type, ready to take part in protein synthesis.
   5 tRNA molecule brings in the correct amino acid to the ribosome.
   1 Unwinding the DNA molecule.
   3 DNA rewinds into double helix structure.
   6 Anti-codon on the tRNA matches with the correct codon on the mRNA and drops off the amino acid.
   7 tRNA leaves the ribosome.
   4 mRNA moves through nuclear pore in the nuclear membrane to the cytoplasm.
   2 mRNA synthesis: Nucleotides added to the growing strand of messenger RNA molecule.

3. The process by which the cell (and therefore the organism) manufactures proteins that may be used as building materials or controlling chemicals.

4. Ribosomal RNA (rRNA), as part of ribosomal structure. Transfer RNA (tRNA). Messenger RNA (mRNA).

5. (a)-(c) in any order:
   - RNA is single stranded, DNA is double stranded.
   - RNA contains the pentose sugar ribose, whereas DNA contains deoxyribose.
   - DNA takes up the twisted double helix whereas RNA does not.
   - RNA has had non-coding codons (introns), which were present in the DNA, removed.
   - Uracil replaces thymine in the code for mRNA.
   - It is mRNA that carries the message of the DNA coding strand in protein synthesis.

6. (a) Transcription (b) Translation

7. (a) UUU to UUC: This change to the third base still codes for the amino acid phenylalanine.
   (b) UUU to UUA: This change to the third base changes the code for the amino acid from phenylalanine to leucine.
   (c) UUU to UUA will change the protein produced.

The Effect of Mutations (page 192)

1. A mutation is any alteration in the base sequence of DNA. The effect of this is the production of a new protein (or other gene product) or the failure to produce a protein. When the mutation involves a change to a regulatory gene (e.g. for production of an enzyme or transcription factor), the consequences can be far-reaching and devastating, because the functions dependent on that regulatory protein also fail.
2. **Somatic mutations** occur in the body (non-gametic or somatic) cells and are not inherited. They may affect an individual within its lifetime. **Gametic mutations** may be inherited and can therefore affect descendants.
3. The mutation does not extend to the seeds (the gametic portion which will be inherited).
4. Organisms such as these have short generation times, so the cumulative effects of mutations over several generations can be feasibly studied. In addition, (especially in bacteria) mutation rates are high and mutations can be induced easily.

For Harm or Benefit? (page 193)

1. (a) A **neutral** (silent) mutation has no effect on the survival and reproduction (fitness) of the individual, whereas a **beneficial** mutation confers a selective advantage in terms of fitness and a **harmful** mutation has a deleterious effect on fitness. Effects apply in the prevailing environment.
   (b) Harmful mutations are the most common, because changes in the normal genetic make-up of an individual are more likely to have a deleterious effect (and cause errors) than be fortuitously beneficial or neutral.
2. Allows people with the mutation to eat food high in cholesterol but not suffer from atherosclerosis.

The Genetic Origins of Cancer (page 194)

1. Cancerous cells have lost control of the genetic mechanisms regulating the cell cycle so that the cells become immortal. They also lose their specialised functions and are unable to perform their roles.

2. The cell cycle is normally controlled by two types of gene: proto-oncogenes, which start cell division and are required for normal cell development, and **tumour-suppressor genes**, which switch cell division off. Tumour suppressor genes will also halt cell division if the DNA is damaged and, if it cannot be repaired, will bring about a programmed cell suicide (apoptosis).

3. Normal controls over the cell cycle can be lost if either the proto-oncogenes or the tumour suppressor genes acquire mutations. Mutations to the proto-oncogenes, with the consequent formation of **oncogenes**, results in uncontrolled cell division. Mutations to the tumour-suppressor genes results in a failure to regulate the cell repair processes and a failure of the cell to stop dividing when damaged.

Oestrogen, Transcription and Cancer (page 195)

1. Oestrogen binds to oestrogen receptors and acts as a transcription factor for the transcription of the AID gene.
2. AID causes somatic hypermutation in the DNA of B cells. This causes them to produce novel copies of antibodies which are produced against a myriad (as yet not encountered) antigens.
3. High levels of oestrogen allow for the greater production of AID because more oestrogen is available to initiate the transcription pathway. Normally, levels of oestrogen fluctuate in the body. In men they are relatively lower, but in women the levels rise just before ovulation. There is a corresponding rise in immunity at this time.
4. AID's normal role is to cause role-driven (purposed) somatic hypermutation in B cells, but it can also cause other mutations. Specifically, it can cause a translocation mutation (of the CD95/Fas gene, a death receptor gene), preventing normal cell death and inducing tumour formation. Continual high levels of oestrogen result in the AID gene being switched on more than is normal, leading to a higher probability of a translocation mutation. This may also explain the link between women on the oral contraceptive pill and their slightly increased risk of cancer.

Herceptin: A Modern Monoclonal (page 196)

1. (a) Overexpression of HER2 causes large amounts of HER2 protein, which causes the cell to divide more often than normal, producing a tumour.
   (b) HER2 protein is a normal component on the surfaces of some cells and is not recognised by the immune system as being of concern. The attachment of a foreign antibody (Herceptin) to HER2 surface proteins alerts the immune system, which then targets the Herceptin (and the HER2protein to which it is attached).
2. (a) Herceptin enables T cells to recognise cells with Her2-Herceptin complexes (i.e cancer-forming cells) and destroy them.
   (b) Herceptin blocks the cell's signalling pathway and prevents the cell from dividing.
3. Monoclonal antibody therapies are called targeted therapies because they target only the cells with the specific antigens for the antibody involved - no others.

Gene Mutations (page 197)

1. A **reading frame shift** occurs when the sequence of bases is offset by one position (by adding or deleting a base). This alters the order in which the bases are grouped as triplets and can severely alter the amino acid sequence.
2. (a) Reading frame shifts and nonsense substitutions.
   (b) They may cause large scale disruption of the coded instructions for making a protein. Either a completely wrong amino acid sequence for part of the protein or a protein that is partly completed (missing amino acids due to an out-of-place terminator codon).
3. Because a reading frame shift severely affects the basic construction of a protein as a set sequence of amino acids, it is unlikely that the protein will be able to carry out its designated role (structural, catalytic, transport). It will lose it biological activity (functionality).

Inherited Metabolic Disorders (page 199)

1. (b) *Gene name*: HBB *Chromosome*: 11
   Mutation type: autosomal recessive. *May be caused by base deletion, base insertion, or gene deletion (severity depends on the mutation).
   (c) *Gene name*: CFTR *Chromosome*: 7
   Mutation type: autosomal recessive. Great range: deletion, missense, nonsense, misplaced terminator codon. Most common is a deletion of 3 nucleotides.
   (d) *Gene name*: IT15 *Chromosome*: 4
   Mutation type: autosomal dominant. Duplication (CAG repeats of varying length).
2. Few or no haemoglobin β chains causes severe anaemia. Frequent blood transfusions are required and this can cause iron accumulation in tissues and organs.
3. Mutations would have arisen in an individual and spread out gradually from that origin. Thus certain genetic disorders tend to have a higher occurrence in certain regions, especially where the population tends to have stayed relatively isolated geographically.

Sickle Cell Mutation (page 200)

1. (a) Bases: 21 (b) Triplets: 7
   (c) Amino acids coded for: 7
2. mRNA: GUG CAC CUG ACU CCU GAG GAG
3. Amino acids: Val His Leu Thr Pro Glu Glu
4. Mutant DNA: CAC GTG GAC TGA GGA CAC CTC
   Type of mutation: Substitution
5. Mutant mRNA:
   GUG CAC CUG ACU CCU GUG GAG
6. Amino acids coded by mutant DNA:
   Val His Leu Thr Pro Val Glu
7. A base substitution causes one amino acid to change in the haemoglobin molecule. This makes the haemoglobin less soluble, and it deforms the red blood cells and results in many circulatory problems.

Cystic Fibrosis Mutation (page 201)

1. (a) mRNA: GGC ACC AUU AAA GAA AAU AUC AUC UUU GGU GGU
   (b) Amino acids: Gly Thr Iso Lys Glu Asn Iso Iso Phe Gly Gly

2. (a) Mutant mRNA: GGC ACC AUU AAA GAA AAU AUC AUC I GGU GGU
   (b) Type of mutation: Triplet deletion.
   (c) Amino acids coded by mutant DNA: Gly Thr Iso Lys Glu Asn Iso Iso I Gly Gly
   (d) Amino acid missing: Phenylalanine (Phe).

3. CF has varying degrees of severity because there are more than 500 mutations of the CF gene. The resulting mutant CFTR protein may not function at all, or it may function only in part, producing a system that is variously effective.

Point Mutation Problems (page 202)

Parts of the transcription and translation process that are affected by the mutation are in **bold**.

1.

Mutant DNA:	AAA	AT**C**	TTT	CTC	CAA	GAT
mRNA:	UUU	UA**G**	AAA	GAG	GUU	CUA
Amino Acids:	Phe	**STOP**	Lys	Glu	Val	Leu

(a) Substitution
(b) Biological significance: The second codon has now been changed to a nonsense or **terminator** codon. Protein synthesis will be prematurely stopped.

2.

Mutant DNA:	AAA	ATG	TTT	CTC	CA**G**	**AT-**
mRNA:	UUU	UAC	AAA	GAG	GU**C**	**UA-**
Amino Acids:	Phe	Tyr	Lys	Glu	Val	?

(a) Deletion (with reading frame shift)
(b) Biological significance: Deletion of a single base at the 14th nucleotide position causes a **'frame shift'**. All amino acids from the deletion point onwards could be different, probably creating a polypeptide chain of no biological function (i.e. it is useless).

3.

Mutant DNA:	AAA	AT**T**	**TTC**	**TCC**	**AG**A	GAT
mRNA:	UUU	UA**A**	**AAG**	**AGG**	**UC**U	CUA
Amino Acids:	Phe	**NON**	**Lys**	**Arg**	**Ser**	Leu

(a) **Deletion** and **insertion** with a partial reading frame shift.
(b) Biological significance: The result is a **temporary frame shift** in the region between the deletion and the insertion. Note that the third codon still codes for lysine. The resulting protein is impaired however, because the second codon now codes for a terminator sequence. This will cause polypeptide formation to be prematurely stopped at that point.

4. **Gene mutations** are small, localised changes in the structure of a DNA strand involving a single gene (e g. deletion, insertion, substitution, reading frame shift). In contrast, **chromosome mutations** involve changes to entire blocks of genes on a chromosome as a result of breaks and rearrangement of chromosome segments (e.g. duplication, inversion, translocation).

Gene Control in Eukaryotes (page 203)

1. (a) **Promoter**: A DNA sequence where RNA polymerase binds and starts transcription.
   (b) **Transcription factors**: These are proteins that recognise and bind to the promoter sequence and to the enhancer sequence and thereby facilitate initiation of transcription.
   (c) **Enhancer sequence**: The DNA sequence to which the transcription factors called activators bind. This binding is important in bringing the activators in contact with the transcription factors bound to the RNA polymerase at the promoter.
   (d) **RNA polymerase**: The enzyme that, with the initial aid of transcription factors, transcribes the gene.
   (e) **Terminator sequence**: Nucleotide sequences at the end of a gene that function to stop transcription.

2. Difference between gene control in prokaryotes and eukaryotes (any one of):
   - Eukaryotic genes are not found as operons; the control sequences may be some distance from he gene to be transcribed.
   - In eukaryotic gene expression, the transcription factors are important; only when the transcription factors are assembled can the gene be transcribed.
   - Eukaryotic gene expression involves the formation of hairpin loop in the DNA which brings the transcription factors and polymerase into contact.

Stem Cells (page 204)

1. (a) They have the ability to self renew while maintaining an undifferentiated state.
   (b) A stem cell has the capacity to differentiate into specialised cells types (potency).

2. Embryonic stem cells are pluripotent and can form over 220 cell types in the three primary germ layers (ectoderm, endoderm, mesoderm). Their potential for medical application is vast as they can theoretically be used to replace most damaged cell and tissue types. Adult stem cells are multipotent and can divided only into a limited number of cell types, mainly those of the blood, heart and nerves. Their medical applications are more limited than ESC, but because there are fewer ethical issues involved ASC are already being used to treat medical problems such as leukaemia.

3. The main purpose of ASC are to maintain and repair the tissue in which they are found. Some examples are:
   - Haematopoietic stem cells give rise to all the types of blood cells, red blood cells, lymphocytes, leukocytes and platelets.
   - Bone marrow stromal cells (mesenchymal stem cells) give rise to a variety of cell types including bone cells (osteocytes), cartilage cells (chondrocytes), fat cells (adipocytes) and connective tissue cells such as tendons.
   - Neural stem cells in the brain can produce nerve cells (neurones) and the non-neuronal cells astrocytes and oligodendrocytes.
   - Epithelial stem cells that line the digestive tract give rise to absorptive cells, globet cells, Paneth cells and enteroendocrine cells.
   - Skin stem cells in the basal layer of the epidermis form keratinocytes which protect the skin. Follicular stem cells at the base of hair follicles give rise to the hair follicle and epidermal cells.

4. Advantages of using embryonic stem cell cloning in tissue engineering (any one of):

   - This technology will provide a disease-free and plentiful supply of (tissue-typed, compatible) cells.
   - Embryonic stem cells have the ability to develop and form all the tissues of the body. Theoretically,

there should be no shortage of specific cell types.
- It will improve the possibility of creating semi-synthetic living organs for use as replacement parts.

Stem Cell Therapy (page 205)

1. ESCs are pluripotent, with the correct stimulus they can differentiate into every type of cell (apart from placental tissue). As their name suggests, their only source is from embryos. ASC are multipotent, they can differentiate into a limited range of tissues, usually related to their tissue of origin. The name ASC is misleading as they are found in umbilical cord blood, children and adults. ASC are found in a limited range of tissue types (e.g. blood, skin, bone marrow).

2. ESC therapies are only undertaken in a limited research capacity. This is because the stem cells are taken from very young embryos (about five days old), which results in the destruction of an embryo. Another argument against ESC research is that it is the beginning of reproductive cloning, which many groups feel very strongly opposed to. ASC therapies are less controversial because the cells are harvested from living donors, and their removal does not cause damage or death to the donor. For this reason ASC therapies are already in use (e.g. bone marrow transplants).
   Note: Currently the source of embryos used in ESC research come from excess embryos created for *in vitro* fertilisation. They are donated with consent to be used for the research.

3. Student's own account. **Note**: Some points of discussion are outlined below:
   Ethical issues to be considered include:
   - The moral implications of using human embryos in an exploitative way, i.e. the embryo from which the stem cell line is derived must have been created for reproductive purposes but is subsequently discarded and must not have had the possibility of developing further as a human being.
   - Informed consent allowing the donation of the embryo and subsequent ownership of it.
   - Policies governing the use of the stem cell lines.

   Technically: Human embryonic stem cell (hESC) research has the potential to allow better understanding of normal cell development and subsequently the possible correction of serious medical conditions such as cancer and birth defects. Another potential application of stem cells is in making replacement cells and tissues for therapeutic purposes e.g. in treating Parkinson's and Alzheimer's diseases, spinal cord injury, stroke, burns, heart disease, diabetes, osteoarthritis and rheumatoid arthritis. Using hESCs poses formidable technical challenges as scientists must learn to control the development of pluripotent stem cells into all the different types of body cells and overcome the threat of rejection by the patient's immune system. Adult stem cell research is not new whereas hESC research is still in its infancy, lacking funding and support, and there may even be laws banning it in some countries.

   See BioLinks under Biotechnology > Applications in Biotechnology > Cloning and Tissue Culture on Biozone's web site for further information on this topic.

Plant Tissue Culture (page 207)

1. The purpose of tissue culture is to produce large numbers of clones (with identical phenotypic and genetic traits as the parent) in a short space of time.

2. (a) A **callus** is a mass of undifferentiated cells.
   (b) Several plant hormones are added to the culture in sequence to stimulate each phase of development.

3. Compared with traditional propagation methods, tissue culture has a number of advantages. Tissue culture enables the production of many clones from a single seed/explant and allows the selection of desirable traits directly from culture. It facilitates rapid propagation, with no wait for seed production and is ideal for plants with long generation times, low seed production, or seeds that are difficult to germinate. Tissue culture also facilitates the international exchange of plants without quarantine and allows researchers to eliminate plant diseases from propagation lines. It is also space saving and overcomes seasonal restrictions to propagation. However, there are several disadvantages to this technology. Tissue culture is very labour intensive and trial and error is necessary to determine the ideal culturing conditions. Cultured plants may be genetically unstable/infertile and, over time, there may be a loss of genetic diversity (see Q4.).

4. Continued culture of a limited number of cloned varieties leads to a change in the genetic composition of the population (the amount of genetic variation decreases). This reduces the amount of variation upon which the gene pool can draw in times of change. This in turn reduces the ability (of the gene pool) to adapt.

What is Genetic Modification? (page 211)

1. Organisms may be genetically modified through:
   - The addition of a foreign gene, e.g. human insulin gene inserted into bacteria or yeast for the commercial production of human insulin.
   - Alteration of an existing gene so that a protein is expressed at a higher rate or in a different way. This GM technique is used in gene therapy.
   - Deletion or inactivation of an existing gene, e.g. the Flavr-Savr tomato which has had its ripening gene switched off. Gene inactivation also produces 'knock-out mice' which are used to study the physiological effects of particular genes.

2. (a) **Gene therapy**: A need/desire to find cures/ treatments for genetic diseases (e.g. cystic fibrosis).
   (b) **Transgenic organisms**: A need to accelerate traditional breeding programmes by direct manipulation of the genome and a desire to improve the usefulness of livestock and crops by increasing production and reducing susceptibility to diseases and pests. There has also been a desire (need?) to produce new protein products by providing novel genes to make plants and animals into biofactories.
   (c) **Plant micropropagation**: A desire for quick, large scale propagation of plant clones with superior traits, a need for disease free specimens, and a need to overcome seasonal growing restrictions.

Applications of GMOs (page 212)

1. Student's own research activity based on information provided in the student workbook or in other texts.

Restriction Enzymes (page 213)

1. (a) **Restriction enzyme**: Enzymes that cut DNA at very precise base sequences (they are able to create sticky end or blunt end junctions). They can be used to remove pieces of DNA from one organism for insertion into a vector or another organism.
   (b) **Recognition site**: The base sequence that a restriction enzyme "recognises" and cuts.
   (c) **Sticky end**: The exposed ends of DNA after a restriction enzyme has cut, leaving a partially unmatched base sequence.
   (d) **Blunt end**: DNA cut leaving no sticky end. May be joined to any other blunt end fragment (not specific).

2. (a) *Eco*RI
   (b) *Escherichia coli* RY13
   (c) GAATTC

3. (a) GGATCC
   (b) Recognition sites: See the diagram below.
   (c) 5 DNA fragments

4. There is a need to have a tool kit of enzymes that allows scientists to cut DNA at any point they wish. The action of such enzymes allows DNA to be manipulated for other recombinant DNA technologies.

Ligation (page 215)

1. (a) **Annealing**: The two single-stranded DNA molecules are recombined into double-stranded form (achieved by H-bonding between complementary bases).
   (b) **DNA ligase**: This enzyme joins two adjacent pieces of DNA by linking nucleotides in the sticky ends.

2. DNA ligase performs the task of linking together the Okazaki fragments during DNA replication.

3. It joins together DNA molecules, while restriction enzymes cut them up.

Gel Electrophoresis (page 216)

1. Purpose of **gel electrophoresis**: To separate mixtures of molecules (proteins, nucleic acids) on the basis of size and other physical properties.

2. (a) The frictional (retarding) force of each fragment's size (larger fragments travel more slowly than smaller ones).
   (b) The strength of the electric field (movement is more rapid in a stronger field).
   Note: The temperature and the ionic strength of the buffer can be varied to optimise separation.

3. The gel is full of pores (holes) through which the fragments must pass. Smaller fragments pass through these pores more easily (with less resistance and therefore faster) than larger ones.

Interpreting Electrophoresis Gels (page 217)

1. Use the mRNA table on the activity page: *The Genetic Code*, to determine the amino acid sequence.
   (a) Synthesised DNA:
   CGT AAG TAC TTG ATC AGA
   GCT CTT CGA AAA TCG
   (b) DNA sample:
   GCA TTC ATG AAC TAG TCT
   CGA GAA GCT TTT AGC
   (c) mRNA:
   CGU AAG UAC UUG AUC AGA
   GCU CUU CGA AAA UCG
   (d) Amino acids:
   Arg Lys Tyr Leu Iso Arg Ala Leu Arg Lys Ser

2. (a) ATG ATC GGC GCT AAA TGT TAA
   (b) ATG CGG AAT TTC CCG GCT TAG
   (c) DNA replication.

3. 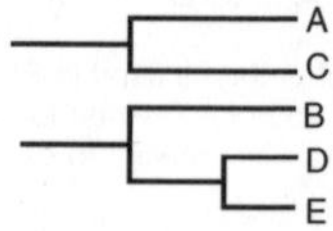

Preparing a Gene for Cloning (page 218)

1. **Restriction enzymes** are used to produce the DNA fragment (often a human gene) that is to be cloned, by isolating it from other DNA and providing it with sticky ends. The same enzymes are used to open up the plasmid or viral DNA into which the DNA fragment is to be inserted.

2. (a) Introns are non-protein coding and removing the makes the gene shorter and therefore easier to insert into vectors and easier for bacteria to translate into the protein produce. In the case of PCR, it means large amounts of non-coding DNA are not made.
   (b) Reverse transciptase catalyses the production of a DNA strand from a strand of RNA.

3. Reverse transcriptase is found in retroviruses (such as HIV) and make a copy of DNA from the viral RNA so that the viral genes can be integrated into (and replicated along with) the host's genome.

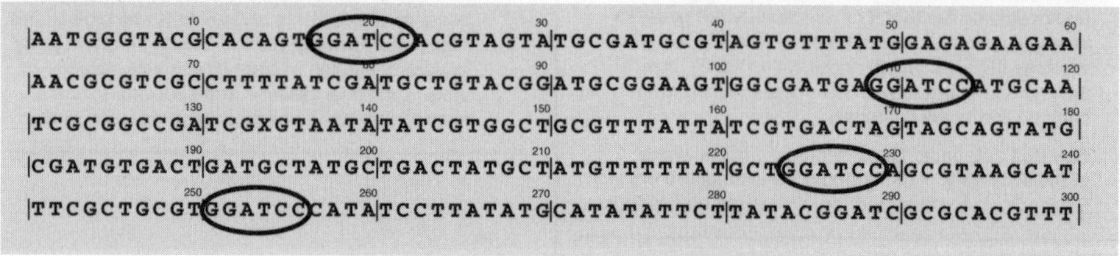

In Vitro Gene Cloning (page 219)

1. To produce large quantities of 'cloned' DNA from very small samples. Large quantities are needed for effective analysis. Very small quantities are often unusable.

2. A double stranded DNA is heated to 98°C for 5 min, causing the two strands to separate. Primers, free nucleotides, and DNA polymerase are added to the sample. The sample is then cooled to 60°C for a few minutes, and the primers anneal to the DNA strands. The sample is incubated and complementary strands are created (by the DNA polymerase) using each strand of the DNA sample as a template. (Incubation temperature depends on the particular polymerase used; it is ~72°C for heat tolerant *Taq* polymerase, but lower for other polymerases). The process is repeated about 25 times, each time the number of templates doubles over the previous cycle.

3. (a) Forensic samples taken at the scene of a crime (e.g. hair, blood, semen).
   (b) Archaeological samples from early human remains.
   (c) Samples taken from the remains of prehistoric organisms preserved in ice, mummified, preserved in amber, tar pits etc.

4. This exercise can be done on a calculator by pressing the 1 button (for the original sample) and then multiplying by 2 repeatedly (to simulate each cycle).
   (a) 1024
   (b) 33 554 432 (33.5 million)

5. (a) It would be amplified along with the intended DNA sample, thereby contaminating the sample and rendering it unusable.
   (b) Sources of contamination (any two of):
   Dirty equipment (equipment that has DNA molecules left on it from previous treatments).
   DNA from the technician (dandruff from the technician is a major source of contamination!)
   Spores, viruses and bacteria in the air.
   (c) Precautions to avoid contamination (any two of):
   Using disposable equipment (pipette tips, gloves).
   Wearing a **head cover** (disposable cap).
   Use of **sterile procedures**.
   Use of **plastic disposable tubes with caps** that seal the contents from air contamination.

6. (a) and (b) any of the following procedures require a certain minimum quantity of DNA in order to be useful: DNA sequencing, gene cloning, DNA profiling, transformation, making artificial genes. Descriptions of these procedures are provided in the workbook.

In Vivo Gene Cloning (page 221)

1. *In vivo* methods make it simpler to produce the protein product because the recipient of the gene (the bacterium) will express the gene as its protein product and this product can then be harvested.

2. One would not use bacteria to clone a gene if the purpose of the gene cloning was simply to amplify the DNA, e.g. for forensic or diagnostic purposes, and protein expression not was required. PCR alone is a simple automated process.

3. The gene is prepared by removal of introns. At the same time, an appropriate vector (e.g. plasmid) is isolated. Both the gene and plasmid are treated with the same restriction enzyme to produce identical sticky ends. The DNA fragments are mixed in the presence of DNA ligase and anneal (DNA ligation).

4. 2 x 24 = 48 replications in twenty four hours. Number of bacteria and therefore plasmids = 2^{48} or 2 multiplied by itself 48 times = 281,474,976,710,656 copies.

5. Recombinant colonies can be identified by their ability to grow on agar with ampicillin but not tetracycline.
   - Grow the bacteria on agar containing ampicillin. All resulting colonies must contain the plasmid.
   - Press a sterile filter paper firmly onto the surface of the agar, taking care to mark the paper's position relative to the agar plate. Press the paper onto another agar plate containing tetracycline and mark the position of the paper relative to the plate. Any colonies that do not grow on this new agar must contain the recombinant DNA (as they have been killed by tetracycline).
   - Match the position of colonies between the first and second agar plates. Those on the first plate that are missing from the second are isolated and cultured.

6. A *gfp* marker is preferable over antibiotic resistance genes because antibiotic resistance genes encourage the undesirable spread of antibiotic resistance through bacterial populations. Apart from this, a gfp marker system is much simpler, as the marked colonies can be quickly identified by fluorescence under UV light.

7. Viruses are used in *in vivo* cloning because they are able to insert DNA into a host's genome. Any altered DNA within them will also be inserted and then copied by the cellular machinery of the host.

Vectors in Transgenesis (page 223)

1. (a) **Transgenesis**: The transfer of genes from one organism (usually another species) to another organism (so that the recipient takes on the characteristics encoded by the foreign DNA).
   (b) **Foreign DNA**: DNA that is not part of the natural genome of a species.

2. The DNA of one organism is introduced (by way of a vector, direct injection, or protoplast fusion) into the genome of another (recipient) organism. The foreign DNA, when expressed, confers new properties on the recipient organism.

3. Examples include (any one):
   - A gene that provides resistance to bacterial disease in rice plants.
   - A gene that improves the nutritional quality of a cereal crop such as rice or wheat.
   - A gene that provides resistance to a crop against herbicide sprays (so that weed control with herbicides will not affect the crop).

4. (a) to (c) any of the following: A need to:
   - Treat genetic diseases in humans.
   - Improve production in livestock (milk, cheese, beef, mutton, wool, leather).
   - Increase pest resistance in crops and livestock.
   - Provide existing crops and livestock with (potentially useful) novel traits (e.g. timber with reduced lignin, cows milk with altered constituents).

- Provide crops with an ability to synthesise their own fertiliser (to reduce dependence on application of agricultural fertilisers).

5. (a) **Advantages** (any two of): • Viruses are good vectors because they are adapted to gain entry into a host's cells • Viruses are very host specific with respect to infection • Viruses can integrate their DNA into that of the host.
   (b) **Disadvantage** (any of): • The host can develop a strong immune response to the viral vector (infection). In patients immune suppressed by their disorder, this severely undermines their health. • Retroviruses infect only dividing cells (uptake may be sporadic or poor). • The inserted genes may only function sporadically because they are not inserted into the chromosome.

6. The purpose of this experiment was simply to show that the technology was viable and that a transgenic animal could be produced.

Human Proteins from GE Bacteria (page 225)

1. (a) High cost (extraction from tissue is expensive).
   (b) Non-human insulin (from pigs or cattle) is different enough from human insulin to cause side effects.
   (c) The extraction methods did not produce pure insulin so the insulin was often contaminated.

2. The insulin is synthesised as two (A and B) nucleotide sequences (corresponding to the two polypeptide chains) because a single sequence is too large to be inserted into the bacterial plasmid. Two shorter sequences are small enough to be inserted (separately) into bacterial plasmids.

3. The β-galactosidase gene in *E.coli* controls the transcription of genes, so the synthetic genes must be tied to that gene in order to be transcribed.

4. (a) Insertion of the gene: The yeast plasmid is larger and could accommodate the entire synthetic nucleotide sequence for the A and B chains as one uninterrupted sequence.
   (b) Secretion and purification: Yeast, being eukaryotic, has secretory pathways that are more similar to humans than those of a prokaryote. Secretion from the cell of the precursor insulin molecules is thus less problematic. Purification would be simplified because removal of β-galactosidase is not required.

5. Mass production of human proteins using GMOs facilitates a low cost, reliable supply for consumer use. The protein (e.g. insulin) is free of contaminants and, because it is a human protein, the side effects of its use are minimised.

6. In the future, gene therapy, where a faulty gene is corrected in the patient, could treat many inherited disorders of metabolism. The use of stem cells, which can differentiate and proliferate in the patient's tissue, may prove the best way to correct genetic disorders.

Golden Rice (page 227)

1. The genes for two different enzymes involved in beta carotene synthesis are taken from two different sources and inserted into the nuclear genome of a rice plant. Expression of the gene under the control of an endosperm specific promoter results in production of beta carotene in the edible portion of the rice plant.

2. The expression of the genes is controlled by a promoter specific to the endosperm, so the genes will only be expressed in that tissue.

3. (a) Production and consumption of beta-carotene rich rice could alleviate or prevent diseases related to vitamin A deficiency (e.g. night blindness and susceptibility to infection as a result of low immunity). Beta carotene is a precursor to vitamin A.
   (b) Improved nutrition through GM rice will be viable only if the diet in targeted regions is also adequate with respect to fat intake. In some impoverished regions this will not be the case, as diet is inadequate across a wide range of food groups, including fat and protein.

Chymosin (page 228)

1. Chymosin (an enzyme) is used to coagulate milk into curds in the production of cheese.

2. Traditional source of chymosin was from the stomachs of young (suckling) calves.

3. (a) **Restriction enzymes** are used to cut the *E. coli* plasmid and isolate the gene for chymosin production (from the calf).
   (b) **DNA ligase** is then used to incorporate the chymosin gene into the plasmid DNA at the point where the restriction enzyme cut.

4. Advantages of using chymosin from GE bacteria:
   (a) The chymosin produced is identical to chymosin from its natural source.
   (b) The chymosin can be produced without the unnecessary slaughter of calves (a welfare issue for many people).
   (c) The chymosin can be produced on demand, in the quantities required. This makes it cost effective.

The Ethics of GMO Technology (page 229)

1. Plants produce pollen which has the potential to be spread in a broadcast fashion (broadcast pollination). This increases the risk that genes (e.g. for herbicide resistance) will be transferred from a GM plant to a weed or other plant. **Note**: Such gene transference has already been demonstrated between plant species. Transfer of sex cells (and therefore genes) between animals in this way does not occur; animal breeding is generally a more precise and difficult process.

2. (a) Advantage: Crop growers could spray a field with herbicide to kill weeds without harming the crop.
   (b) Problem: Herbicide resistance may be spread to weed plants by viral or bacterial vectors that infect plants. Encourages overuse of herbicide chemicals.

3. (a) Advantage: Ability to grow tropical food crops in regions that could not previously do so.
   (b) Problem: Such plants in a new environment may

become pest species. Undeveloped economies that rely on tropical cash crops may suffer as a result of competition from economically strong countries.

4. (a) Advantage: Will allow regions that are poor in agricultural production to produce crops.
   (b) Problem: Such plants in a new environment may become pest species. Disturbs natural wetland habitats, probably resulting in the loss of wetland and marsh native species.

5. In any order:
   (a) Enhancing wool production in sheep (yield and/or wool quality).
   (b) Use of livestock animals as biofactories by producing useful proteins in their milk (especially cattle, but also sheep and goats).

6. The widespread use of antibiotic marker genes in food crops for human consumption or stock food may give rise to antibiotic resistant strains of pathogenic bacteria which affect humans and stock animals. Restrained use of antibiotics is now considered essential in preventing large scale development of antibiotic resistance.

7. (a) Introduces nitrogen fixing ability in non-legumes thereby reducing the need for nitrogen fertilisers.
   (b) The bacterium would prevent attack on the seeds by pathogenic bacteria and fungi.

8. **Note**: This question was not intended to imply that ethical or moral concerns are any less real or valid than biological ones. It was merely an exercise in identifying the nature of the biological concerns.
   (a) Some points for discussion are:
   - That the GM product and/or the GMO could have some unwanted harmful effect on humans or other organisms.
   - That the genetic modification would spread uncontrollably into other organisms (breeding populations of the same or different species).
   - Consumer choice is denied unless adequate labelling protocols are in place. If everything contains GM products, there is no consumer choice in this area.
   - General fear of what is not understood (fear of real or imagined consequences).
   - Objections on the grounds that it is ethically and morally wrong to tamper with the genetic make-up of an organism.
   - Generation of monopolies where large companies control the rights to seed supplies & breeding stock.

   (b) Those that pose a real biological threat are:
   - Amongst plant GMOs, the indiscriminate spread of foreign genes.
   - Unusual physiological reactions e.g. allergies, to novel proteins.
   - Some animal rights issues may be justified if genetic modification causes impaired health.

Gene Therapy (page 231)

1. (a) The principle of gene therapy is to correct a genetic disorder of metabolism by correction, replacement, or supplementation of a faulty gene with a corrected version. **Note**: Some techniques involve culturing corrected cells *ex vivo*. Injection of corrected cells into the patient relieves the symptoms of the disorder but does cure it.
   (b) Medical areas where gene therapy might be used: Inherited genetic disorders of metabolism, cancers and other non-infectious acquired diseases, and infectious diseases (e.g. viral infections).

2. Transfection of (and correction of the genes in) **germline cells** allows the genetic changes to be inherited. **Note**: In this way, a heritable disorder can be corrected so that future generations will not carry the faulty gene(s). Transfection of **somatic cells** only corrects those cells for their lifetime.

3. **Gene amplification** is used to make multiple copies of the normal (corrective) allele.

4. GM stem cells offer longer lasting treatment because the cells will continue proliferating and the therapeutic role will continue as long as the cell line continues. Once a transformed (corrected) somatic cell has reached the end of its life, its therapeutic role ends.

Vectors for Gene Therapy (page 232)

Correction: The diagram panel "Plasmid Vectors" has a pointer to the plasmid that should have been removed. There is no missing information.

1. (a) Viruses are good vectors because they are adapted to gain entry into a host's cells and integrate their DNA into that of the host.
   (b) Viral vectors can cause problems because (two of):
   - The host can develop a strong immune response to the viral infection. In patients disadvantaged (immune suppressed) by their disorder, this could severely undermine their health.
   - Retroviruses infect only dividing cells.
   - Viruses may not survive if attacked by the host's immune system.
   - If they do not integrate into the chromosome, the inserted genes may only function sporadically.
   - The genes may integrate randomly into chromosomes and disrupt the functioning of normal genes (this occurred recently in retroviral vectors used in SCID gene therapy patients).

2. (a) If a therapeutic gene is integrated into the chromosome, it has a better chance of functioning properly in the long term, and being stable (not degraded) in the cell.
   (b) When it integrates into the host's (patient's) chromosome, the gene has the potential to disrupt normally functioning genes (see 1(b) above). **Note**: in recent gene therapy trials in SCID patients, retroviral vectors integrated preferentially into currently active genes.

3. (a) Naked DNA is unstable because it is recognised as foreign and is easily degraded by the normal clean-up mechanisms occurring in the host's tissues (phagocytes etc.). Uptake by cells is inefficient and, once within the cell, the DNA is still at risk of degradation by lysosomes.
   (b) Liposomes offer greater stability because they are formulated so that they are recognised by the host's cell receptors and they target these receptors (so are more directed). They are therefore less likely to be degraded in the tissues.

Gene Delivery Systems (page 233)

1. (a) **CF symptoms**: Disruption of gland function including the pancreas, intestinal glands, biliary

tree, sweat glands, and bronchial glands. Infertility occurs in males and females. Disruption of lung function produces the most obvious symptom; the accumulation of thick, sticky mucus in the lungs and associated breathing difficulties.

(b) CF has been targeted because the majority of cases are the result of a gene defect involving the loss of only one triplet (three nucleotides). In theory, correction of this one gene should not be difficult.

(c) Correction rate has been low (25%), and the effects of correction have been short lived and the benefits quickly reversed. These problems are related to the poor survival of the viral vector in the body and the sporadic functioning of the gene because it is not integrated into the host's (human) chromosome. Patients suffer problems with immune reaction to the vector. In one patient, treatment was fatal.

2. (a) **Vector**: Adenoviruses.
Note: potential problems (not required): Gene may function only sporadically when not integrated into the host's chromosome. Adenoviruses have poor survival in the body and are quickly destroyed by the immune system. As a result, corrective rates are low and the effects of the corrective gene are short lived. Patients may show various adverse reactions, as a result of their immune response to the vector.

(b) **Vector**: Liposomes
Note: potential problems (not required): Liposomes are less efficient than viruses at transferring genes, so corrective rates are lower than for viral vectors.

3. (a) X-linked SCID is caused by a mutation to a gene on the X chromosome that encodes for the common gamma chain. ADA SCID is caused by a defective gene that codes for the enzyme adenosine deaminase.

(b) The vector used in the treatment of SCID is a gutted retrovirus (a retorvirus with its natural genetic material removed to make room for the coorective gene being transferred).

4. Gene therapy for cystic fibrosis is targeted at the lungs using either an adenovirus or a liposome delivered via the airways. SCID is treated using a retrovirus introduced to the patient's own bone marrow and the returned to the patient.

5. (a) Chance of interfering with essential gene function: When an essential gene function is affected by gene therapy in somatic cells, the individual will be affected. There may be a chance of corrective therapy in that person's lifetime. When the change affects germline cells, all descendants of the treated individual have a chance to inherit the disrupted gene, so a second heritable defect is created.

(b) Misuse of the therapy to selectively alter phenotype: Alteration of somatic cells to selectively alter one's phenotype is (presumably) a matter of one's own choice; it may benefit that person in their own lifetime, but will not affect subsequent generations. When these selective changes affect the germline cells, then they are heritable and the alteration is not necessarily limited to one individual. This poses the problem of genetic selection and eugenics, and all their consequent ethical dilemmas.

DNA Chips (page 236)

1. Purpose: To determine the presence or sequence of genes in a sample, and the expression or activity level of those genes.

2. (a) The gene probes making up the microarray fluoresce when cDNA binds to them (called nucleic acid hybridisation). This indicates that the RNA product has been expressed in the cell it was taken from. A quantitative amount of gene activity can be computer generated.

(b) Reverse transcriptase makes a single-stranded copy (cDNA) of the RNA extracted from a cell.

3. (a) Genes that turned red in the microarray (2 and 24) were over-expressed and therefore the most antibiotic resistant genes from the bacteria.

(b) New antibiotics would be designed to silence these genes that are antibiotic resistant. Alternatively, new antibiotics could also be developed to affect those bacterial genes that are not antibiotic resistant (e.g. genes 4, 17, and 22).

4. They have evolved from Southern Blotting techniques where fragmented DNA is attached to a substrate and then probed with a known gene or fragment. Many different DNA probes are incorporated into a DNA chip. Each spot on the chip has thousands-to-millions of copies of a probe and the colour of the spot allows a quantitative read-out of a particular gene's activity in a cell. Advantages include identifying which genes are expressed in a particular tissue and to what extent.

5. The information gained from the microarray could be used to identify which tissue was cancerous and to what degree the cancer was present. This would then enable specialists to advise the best treatment for a particular cancer.

Genome Analysis (page 239)

1. (a) **Genome mapping**: Locates the exact position of all the genes on the various chromosomes. Produce genetic and physical maps of varying resolution.

(b) **Genome sequencing**: Determines the precise nucleotide (base) sequence for each gene. From this can be determined the gene product (protein).

2. A **clone library** (also known as a gene library) is a collection of cloned DNA sequences representative of the entire genome of the organism under study. The cloned DNA sequences reside in the accessory chromosomes of other organisms (yeast, bacteria) into which they are placed (each type of fragment resides in a separate culture). In contrast, a **subclone library** is a collection of much smaller DNA fragments (1500-5000 bp), each inserted into a plasmid vector and cloned.

3. (a) **Restriction enzymes**: The genome is cut up using restriction enzymes in preparation for creating a clone library and subclone library.

(b) **Ligation**: DNA fragments are inserted into vectors using DNA ligation to create a clone library and subclone library.

(c) **PCR**: The positions of DNA markers on each fragment are determined using PCR (and gel electrophoresis).

(d) **Gel electrophoresis**: The positions of DNA markers on a fragment are determined using gel electrophoresis (and PCR). Gel electrophoresis is also used to sequence each small DNA fragment to determine the exact base sequence.

4. DNA markers provide genetic landmarks along the length of DNA being sequenced. These are used to assemble the sequences for each of the fragments in the correct order.

The Human Genome Project (page 241)

1. **HGP**: Aims to map the entire base sequence of every chromosome in the human cell (our genome), to identify all genes in the sequence, determine what they express (protein produced), and determine the precise role of every gene on the chromosomes.
   HGDP: The HGDP aims to map the differences in genomes between different racial and ethnic groups.

2. Genomic differences on the basis of race could be misused for discriminatory purposes.

3. (a) **Medical** (any of the following):
   - Will identify the location and sequence for up to 4000 known genetic diseases, opening up opportunities for drug therapy.
   - Will provide the information to enable the production of human proteins to correct metabolic deficiencies.
   - Will open up the possibility of gene therapy for many genetic diseases.
   - Will enable the development of new therapeutic drugs to block metabolic pathways.
   - With greater knowledge, emphasis will shift from treatment of disease to better diagnosis and prevention of disease.
   - Screening for genetic predisposition to disease.
   - The ability to sequence quickly and directly will revolutionise mutation research (direct study of the link between mutagens and their effects).

   (b) **Non-medical** (any of the following):
   - What we learn about human genetics will enable improvement of livestock management.
   - Provides a knowledge base that is a key to understanding the structure, function, and organisation of DNA in chromosomes.
   - Provides the basis for comparative studies with other organisms (e.g. for taxonomic purposes).
   - Provides a greater understanding of human evolution and anthropology.
   - Facilitates developments in forensics.

4. **Proteomics** is the study (including identification) of the protein products of identified genes. It relies on the knowledge gained by the HGP, but will ultimately provide the most useful information.

5. Student's own discussion. Suggestions for each issue listed in the table (pros and cons) are as follows:
   - Rights of third parties:

   (a) They should have the genetic information in order to make an informed decisions (about insurance premiums etc.) to the benefit of those with "favourable" genetic test results.
   (b) They should be denied the information because they could use it to unfairly discriminate against people with "unfavourable" genetic test results.

   - No treatment, therefore the knowledge is pointless:

   (a) Although there may be no treatment initially, treatment may become available and knowledge of genetic predisposition will allow informed decisions to be made at short notice if necessary.
   (b) Knowing that one has a disease and cannot do anything about it could create emotional problems for many people.

   - High costs of tests:

   (a) Although the costs are high, the knowledge is important to a person's health and to medical research generally and is justifiable.
   (b) If costs are not met by public funds, the high costs will preclude those individuals who cannot personally afford them.

   - Genetic information is hereditary:

   (a) Knowledge of an inherited disease or disorder lets family members assess their risks when planning their own lives.
   (b) Family members may feel forced to not have children if their risk of an inherited disorder is high.

Investigating Genetic Biodiversity (page 243)

1. A **proteinase** enzyme dissolves the tissues of the springtails to release the DNA from the cells.

2. (a) *Taq* polymerase binds to the DNA primers and synthesises the complementary strands of DNA.
   (b) Nucleotides are added to the PCR mixture because the polymerase requires the free nucleotides to synthesise the complementary DNA strands.
   (c) The high temperature (92°C) separates the strands of DNA. The lower temperature (45°C) causes the primers to anneal to each DNA strand. The sample is then incubated at 72°C because this is the optimum working temperature for the Taq polymerase (a thermophilic bacterial enzyme) which synthesises the complementary DNA strands.

3. (a) The **negative** will be any substance devoid of DNA, e.g. water or some chemical solution blank.
   (b) The **reference** (also called the ladder) provides a reference position for fragments of known length to which the unknown sample fragments can be compared. The fragment length in the sample can then be determined.

4. (a) A point mutation (gene mutation involving a change to one nucleotide).
   (b) The point mutation has occurred to the first base of a codon. Unlike mutations to the third base, which are less likely to change the amino acid coded for, a change to the first base will cause a change in the amino acid. Another amino acid will form part of the polypeptide chain made from this gene.

DNA Profiling Using PCR (page 245)

1. STRs (microsatellites) are non-coding nucleotide sequences (2-6 base pairs long) that repeat themselves many times over (repeats of up to 100X). The human genome has numerous different STRs; equivalent sequences in different people vary considerably in the numbers of the repeating unit. This property can be used to identify the natural variation found in every person's DNA since every person will have a different combination of STRs of different repeat length, i.e. their own specific genetic profile.

2. (a) **Gel electrophoresis**: Used to separate the DNA fragments (STRs) according to size to create the fingerprint or profile.
   (b) **PCR**: Used to make many copies of the STRs. Only the STR sites are amplified by PCR, because the primers used to initiate the PCR are very specific.

3. (a) Extract the DNA from sample. Treat the tissue with chemicals and enzymes to extract the DNA, which is then separated and purified.
   (b) Amplify the microsatellite using PCR. Primers are used to make large quantities of the STR.
   (c) Run the fragments through a gel to separate them. The resulting pattern represents the STR sizes for that individual (different from that of other people).

4. To ensure that the number of STR sites, when compared, will produce a profile that is effectively unique (different from just about every other individual). It provides a high degree of statistical confidence when a match occurs.

Forensic Applications of DNA Profiling (page 247)

1. Lane A acts a control or calibration lane containing fragment s of DNA of known length.

2. Profiles of everyone involved must be completed to compare their DNA to any DNA found at the scene and therefore eliminate (or possibly implicate!) them as suspects.

3. The alleged offender is not guilty. The alleged offender's DNA profile does not appear in the DNA collected at the crime scene nor does it appear in the DNA database. In fact profile E's DNA is found at the scene.

4. Each individual whale has its own DNA profile. By profiling the whale meat it is possible to identify how many whales were killed by simply counting the number of different profiles. It can then be told if whale meat sold as coming from one whale in fact came from two or more.

Genetic Counselling (page 248)

1. **Carrier screening** would allow the parents to ascertain the risk of conceiving a child with the family genetic disorder. This information could then be used to explore alternative methods of conceiving a child that is at lower risk of inheriting the disorder.

2. (a) Huntington disease persists because those with the mutation are able to reproduce and pass on the disorder before its effects are expressed.
   (b) Presymptomatic genetic testing would allow carriers of the Huntingtin gene to make informed choices when considering starting a family.